a **good** catch

Best wishes
Jill
Lambert

Sustainable

SEAFOOD RECIPES

from Canada's

Top Chefs

JILL LAMBERT

a **good** catch

David Suzuki Foundation

GRE**Y**STONE BOOKS

Douglas & McIntyre Publishing Group

VANCOUVER/TORONTO/BERKELEY

To my husband, Justin Smallbridge, and our boys, Henry and Spencer.

Greystone Books
A division of Douglas & McIntyre Ltd.
2323 Quebec Street, Suite 201
Vancouver, British Columbia
Canada V5T 4S7
www.greystonebooks.com

David Suzuki Foundation
2211 West 4th Avenue, Suite 219
Vancouver, British Columbia
Canada V6K 4S2

Library and Archives Canada Cataloguing in Publication
Lambert, Jill, 1962–
A good catch : sustainable seafood recipes from Canada's top chefs / Jill Lambert.
Includes index.
Co-published by: David Suzuki Foundation.

ISBN 978-1-55365-385-1

1. Cookery (Seafood). 2. Sustainable fisheries. I. David Suzuki
Foundation II. Title.
TX747.L338 2008   641.6'92   C2008-904112-7

Editing by Lucy Kenward
Copyediting by Pam Robertson
Jacket and text design by Naomi MacDougall
Jacket and interior illustrations by Naomi MacDougall
Printed and bound in Canada by Friesens
Printed on acid-free paper that is forest friendly (100% post-consumer recycled paper) and has been processed chlorine free
Distributed in the US by Publishers Group West

We gratefully acknowledge the financial support of the Canada Council for the Arts, the British Columbia Arts Council, the Province of British Columbia through the Book Publishing Tax Credit, and the Government of Canada through the Book Publishing Industry Development Program (BPIDP) for our publishing activities.

Contents

Foreword

My earliest memories from childhood are of going camping and fishing with my father. And fish have remained a central part of my life ever since.

As a young boy growing up in London, Ontario, I was an outsider. Fish kept me out of trouble and interested in the world. If I was too scared to ask a girl out on a date, I could at least go fishing—and I spent hours in local waters trying to entice these fascinating creatures to take my hook.

Fishing continued to connect me to nature as well as being a source of enjoyment, peace, and food as I went through school, started a family, and built a career. Later in life, I learned from the First Nations in British Columbia about the central role wild salmon have played in their culture and spirituality throughout thousands of years of rich history.

More recently, work supported by my foundation has brought to light scientific evidence of the essential role salmon serve in accumulating critical nutrients from the ocean, which are then spread through the entire ecosystem of the Pacific temperate rain forest and even fertilize the mighty trees.

Fish and the waters they inhabit sustain us in all kinds of ways. Obviously, they provide food and generate economic activity, they connect and support ecosystems, and they are part of larger marine systems that regulate weather and absorb greenhouse gases to slow global warming.

But fish and the oceans, lakes, and rivers where they live are in trouble these days, and it hurts me to see it. Stocks are declining because of overfishing, habitats are being destroyed by bottom trawling or urban sprawl, oceans are being acidified from climate change, and pollution is killing lakes and streams. All of which threaten these animals that we rely on for so much.

The problems are many, but we as individuals *can* help. We can make wise choices about what seafood we eat, and we can translate that care into action. By choosing to buy fish that are abundant, well managed, and caught or farmed in ways that do not destroy the environment, we can make a difference: we can reduce the demand for fish that aren't sustainable, we can put pressure on industries to do better, and we can tell governments that we want them to take care of these precious creatures and their habitat.

Please join me in translating the sustainable-seafood recipes in this book, lovingly provided by chefs and fish lovers from across Canada, into wonderful meals. And I hope that, in between meals, you also take the time to tell the folks who work at your local grocery stores and restaurants, as well as your elected representatives, how much we need their help to make sustainable seafood the only fish in the sea. So now, enjoy.

David Suzuki

Acknowledgements

My profound thanks to:

the chefs, for giving their recipes

Dr. David Suzuki, for his support of this project and for his leadership

the multi-talented Julie Marr, chief recipe tester, adventure fish shopper, and problem solver

Jennifer Danter, who created a clear and consistent recipe manuscript

Alison Lambert, Susie Findlay, and Linda Yorke, for recipe testing

Lesley Chesterman, Sadie Beaton, Tina Pittaway, Leah Mann, and Jennifer Cockrall-King, for chef contacts and recipes

Jay Ritchlin, Bill Wareham, Dominic Ali, and Scott Wallace of the David Suzuki Foundation; Taina Uitto of SeaChoice Canada; Susanna Fuller of the Ecology Action Centre, and Robert Campbell, for the information they provided about fish and sustainability

Rob Sanders, Nancy Flight, and Lucy Kenward of Greystone Books, for bringing this book about

Evan Pyle, for his interest and support

my father, Doug Lambert, for his help and support

my mother, Beverly Lambert, for taking me fishing

my uncle, Sonny Nelson, for sharing his knowledge and his wonderful dinners. Thanks for all the great fish!

Introduction

A NOTE ON FISH: To keep this text simple, I've used the word "fish" to cover a multitude of categories, including saltwater and freshwater fin fish as well as shellfish.

I love to eat fish. I come from a family with a good seafood pipeline: lots of fresh salmon, smoked salmon, halibut, crab, and prawns come to our table from my mother's brother, Sonny Nelson. He keeps a skiff in a marina near his waterfront home in West Vancouver, and he fishes in the waters between Point Grey and Bowen Island. He's an experienced and skillful fisherman, and a genuinely lucky guy: we call him "the fishin' magician" because he can haul it in when everyone else is getting skunked.

Sonny is more than a casual sport fisherman; in fact, he spent his working life in the fishing business, which for him was the family firm. His dad (my grandfather) was Norman Nelson, who started up Nelson Brothers Fisheries in 1928 with his brother Richard. Nelson Brothers was a fish-packing company with canneries along the West Coast, and the brothers produced the Paramount brand of canned salmon and sold it all over Canada.

Norman Nelson was born in 1890 near Tromsø, Norway, some three hundred kilometres north of the Arctic Circle. He quit school at age fourteen to fish with a hand line over the side of an open boat in the North Sea. Countless generations of Nelsons fished like this as a way of life, and these fishermen and their families depended on what the sea would provide for them. So, for me, eating seafood is a family tradition.

Over time, I grew to realize the special significance of fish. Most of the seafood I eat is wild. Fish is the only wild protein in most people's diet. When we eat it, we're taking in some of the beautiful natural world that surrounds us.

FISHING ON BORROWED TIME

For all of us these days, eating fish is more complicated than it used to be. To satisfy growing demand, we are catching fish and shellfish faster than they can reproduce, pushing their populations lower and lower. According to the Monterey Bay Aquarium, one of the world's leading authorities in marine research, education, and conservation, ocean fishers increased their catch 400 per cent between 1950 and 1994 by doubling the number of boats and using more effective fishing gear.

There's a limit to how much the ocean can produce and how much of it we can catch. We reached that limit in 1989, when the world's catch levelled off at just over eighty-two million metric tons of fish per year. The sustainability of the global fish harvest is a very serious issue: while in North America we may choose to include fish in our weekly meal plan, fish is essential to the diet of many people in the developing world. It's estimated that for one in every five people, fish is the primary source of protein. If fish become too scarce, millions of people will have to find another source of protein in their diet. To avert this crisis, we have to change the way we fish.

Although change on a large scale will require government action, anyone who eats fish can be part of the solution. By paying more attention to the kinds of fish on our plates, to where and how they were caught, we can affect the market and work to move it in the right direction.

MAKING GOOD FISH DECISIONS

We have the power to choose fish that have been harvested in a sustainable manner. Sustainability simply means doing things in such a way that we can continue to do them in the future. It joins environmental goals with the goals of development. Sustainably harvested seafood, freshwater fish, and shellfish are caught in a way that doesn't harm the environment that produces them and doesn't result in other animals, including mammals, being killed and thrown away. It's also really important to choose seafood that comes from abundant stocks. Some stocks are so depleted they are endangered.

With many different variables to consider, making good choices can be tricky. The best place to begin is with some general guidelines, such as those established by SeaChoice Canada. SeaChoice was created by Sustainable Seafood Canada and is comprised of the Ecology Action Centre, the Living Oceans Society, the Sierra Club of Canada, the Canadian Parks and Wilderness Society, and the David Suzuki Foundation.

SeaChoice has created a wallet card that helps people make sustainable seafood choices. The card is divided into three sections—"Best Choice," "Some Concerns," and "Avoid"—with a list of corresponding species. Most species appear in only one category. However, a species *can* be listed in more than one category if it is caught using a number of fishing methods or if it is found in several specific areas. For example, Pacific cod that has been harvested by long-line, jig, or pot is a "Best Choice" option; Atlantic cod is listed as "Avoid" no matter how it's caught.

The card is a good place to start, but the next move is yours. Speak up! Try to learn as much as possible about the fish you buy. The next time you buy fish at the market, or order it in a restaurant, ask a few questions.

The first question is: What species is this? It's important to be precise, because in some cases, one species of a common fish or shellfish is a problem whereas another is not. For example, bluefin tuna is severely overfished and is not a good choice. Albacore tuna, however, is a great choice; stocks are well managed and currently abundant.

The second question is: Where was it caught? Knowing where the fish comes from will help you distinguish between a good choice and a bad one. For example, British Columbia prawns are a much better choice than warm-water prawns. Also, it's usually a better bet to buy fish that's harvested close to home, if possible, than to buy seafood that has travelled a long distance.

The third question is: How was it caught? Some fishing methods are very destructive to the environment, others are fine. For example, trolling is a responsible fishing method that doesn't damage the environment. Other fishing methods, such as purse seining, can be a problem due to "bycatch": fish and marine mammals that are caught unintentionally by fishing gear meant for other species. For example, nets intended to target tuna can also catch other species such as dolphins, sharks, and turtles, which are tossed out, dead or dying.

The people who sell you your fish may not have this information, but if enough of us ask for it, perhaps vendors will be motivated to ask their suppliers and choose to sell sustainably harvested product. When that happens, the market can shift toward more responsible and sustainable choices. If all fish were labelled with the species name, place of origin, and method of harvest, making good decisions would be a lot easier.

USING A GOOD CATCH

When I first saw the SeaChoice card, I was dismayed to see that red snapper was on the "Avoid" list. At the time, I was eating snapper at least once a week, so I realized I was going to have to change my habits. Looking over the "Best Choice" category, I saw some names of familiar species and some that I'd never eaten before. I decided to learn to cook the various fish on the "Best Choice" list—and that's what led to this book.

I asked chefs from across Canada to share recipes that use these species, and the chefs responded. I tried recipes for octopus and geoduck and sardines and tilapia—food that I had never cooked before. Of course, I quickly came to realize there are great choices beyond the more typical salmon and halibut. Now, I cook salmon in celebration and really appreciate when I have it. For my everyday meals, though, I choose from many different species, now that I know what to do with them.

The recipes in this book use fish and shellfish from the "Best Choice" category; I've also included some from the category marked "Some Concerns." Each recipe includes the sustainability of the main ingredients used in that dish, and longer profiles at the back of the book detail particular issues concerning the sustainability of individual species.

As our awareness grows and the climate changes, some species are bound to become more sustainable, others less. Three great sources of information are *State of the Catch: A Professional's Guide to Sustainable Seafood,* published by the David Suzuki Foundation (www.davidsuzuki.org/files/Oceans/StateoftheCatch.pdf), Sustainable Seafood Canada's SeaChoice program (www.seachoice.org), and the Monterey Bay Aquarium Seafood Watch program (www.mbayaq.org). You can use these resources to stay up to date as the issues of sustainability evolve. Please visit my Web site, www.agoodcatch.org, for more information about sustainable fish and lots of photographs of dishes made from the recipes in this book.

Sustainable Alternatives for Popular Species—Choosing Good Fish Over Bad

IF YOU USUALLY CHOOSE...	TRY SWITCHING TO THIS INSTEAD
farmed salmon	wild salmon
Chilean sea bass	halibut, sablefish
monkfish	lobster, halibut, sablefish, Pacific cod
orange roughy	tilapia, haddock, catfish
red snapper	tilapia, sablefish, Pacific cod
sole or flounder	tilapia, catfish
bluefin tuna	albacore or yellowtail tuna, swordfish
wild clams	farmed clams
wild mussels, oysters	farmed mussels, oysters
tiger prawns or tropical prawns from Asia	cold-water shrimp or prawns, such as sidestripe shrimp, spot prawns, or Chedabucto Bay shrimp

Choosing, Preparing, and
Storing Fish and Seafood

Buying good fish and seafood can be a challenge. The counters at many grocery stores put a lot of distance between the product and the customer, so it can be hard to know if the food is fresh—you can't smell it or see it up close. It's the same for fish and shellfish packaged in plastic wrap and Styrofoam. Sometimes when you unwrap the package, the food is clearly not fresh.

I think some stores label seafood as fresh when it's been previously frozen. Even worse, some producers treat fish and shellfish with chemicals to keep them fresh longer; this can denature the protein, which makes the texture mushy. It's so disappointing when this happens.

To avoid such problems, I buy from stores I trust. Finding these places involves some trial and error, but it's worth the effort. I prefer to buy seafood right off the boat, from the hands of the person who caught it. Of course, that's not always possible. I also buy frozen fish and shellfish—it's often a good choice, especially if it's been flash-frozen at sea and vacuum-packed. In the old days, fishing boats carried their catch packed in ice, which meant the boats could be out at sea for only a certain length of time before the seafood went off. Now, many fish are frozen at sea, which preserves the freshness very well, so the boats can stay out longer.

Shipping seafood by air to meet the demands of sophisticated consumers has become a common practice, and special runs of fish and shellfish often appear on restaurant menus in distant cities. For example, it's not uncommon to see Copper River salmon from Alaska or oysters from Fanny Bay or Cortes Island, British Columbia, available as far away as New York. However, the environmental impact of shipping by plane is substantial, and a fish harvested sustainably may become an unsustainable choice because of the impact of transportation.

In the past few years, eating "local" has become a popular concept. Growing awareness of the enormous distance some food travels before it lands in our grocery stores has sparked interest in buying food that's produced closer to home. Some people set geographical limits to the food they're willing to consume; so-called "locavores" will only eat food grown within a certain distance (such as one hundred miles) of their homes. Although this commitment to eating local foods makes good environmental sense, it's not necessary to reject all imported products. Occasionally, a species respectfully harvested, processed in a highly energy-efficient fish-processing plant on the other side of the world, and transported by container ship to market still represents a sustainable choice—if you can figure out this "chain of custody."

I try to choose seafood that has the lowest environmental impact in terms of where it's caught, how it's moved to market, and what it means for stocks in general. If eating local means eating farmed salmon, it's not a sustainable choice. It's a bit of a balancing act. I just do the best I can.

When I'm buying fresh whole fish, I want to take a good look at it first. I'll ask the vendor to take it out of the case and show it to me. Choose fish that looks moist and firm. It should smell fresh, not overly "fishy"—if it smells unpleasant or like ammonia, don't buy it! If the head is on the fish, the eyes should be clear and bright, not cloudy.

Fish fillets should be firm, shiny, and moist. If the fish is wrapped in plastic, touch it very gently; the flesh should bounce back. Again, if there's a strong unpleasant odour, don't buy it.

Fresh shellfish in the shell, such as mussels, clams, and oysters, should be alive when you buy them. The shells should be tightly closed; if they're open, they should snap shut if you tap them. If you buy shucked oysters, they should look firm and shiny, and there should be no unpleasant odour. Make sure they are cold, not stored at room temperature. Scallops are more often sold shucked, and they are graded according to size; for example, U/10 indicates large scallops, meaning that ten or fewer scallops will add up to a pound. Choose the size that will work best for your recipe.

Prawns and shrimp are often sold with their shells; the shells should be shiny and tight. Avoid broken or cracked shells, and, again, check that there's no strong smell. Sometimes prawns and shrimp are graded by size and weight; you may see them priced according to how many make up a pound or a kilogram, with the largest being the most expensive. For example, you may see prawns listed as 20/30, which means that somewhere between twenty and thirty prawns will make up one pound. Choose the size that works best for your recipe, and remember, if you're buying prawns and shrimp in the shell, some of the heavier ones have egg sacs that you may not enjoy eating.

Packaged fish and shellfish are labelled with standard information required by the Canada Food Inspection Agency, including the name of the species, the country of origin, and information about other ingredients. The label will also have a "best before" date, which lets you know how long the product will last. It may also contain the statement "keep refrigerated." It's in your best interest to heed these instructions.

KEEPING FISH AND SHELLFISH FRESH

I go to a lot of trouble to buy quality fish, so when I get it home I want to keep it as fresh as I can. I learned from my fisherman uncle, Sonny Nelson, that keeping it on ice is a really good idea. When he was buying fish on the halibut exchange in Prince Rupert, he'd see a catch that was twenty days old come in from the Bering Sea packed on ice and still perfectly good.

When Sonny has a nice fresh fish, he cleans it, packs it in ice, and keeps it on his porch in a cooler. The melting ice washes the bacteria off the fish and the temperature stays consistent at 0°C. Of course, you'll need to use lots of ice and replenish it as it melts, but this method will keep a whole fish fresh for much longer. If you've got a smaller piece of fish, you can pack a small plastic container full of ice, bury the fish in the ice, and keep the whole thing in the fridge. Again, the ice will help to keep the fish a lot fresher.

It's best to cook and eat shellfish within twenty-four hours of purchase. If you need to store shellfish overnight, keep it in the original packaging in the refrigerator until you're ready to use it. Live crabs can be refrigerated for a few hours; the cold temperature will reduce a crab's activity and generally makes it easier to handle while it's still alive. Be careful, though, because the crab may move around. (You might want to wrap it loosely in a tea towel before you put it in the fridge.) I usually clean and cook crab immediately after I buy it. Cooked crab should be eaten within twenty-four hours, as the flesh starts to break down quickly.

PREPARING FISH

If the piece of fish you're preparing has skin, you may need to scale it. Remove the scales by scraping the back of a knife against the skin under cold running water. (It is a sign of freshness if the scales are difficult to remove.)

Most fish can be cooked on the bone and filleted after cooking. Almost any meat tastes better cooked on the bone. Fish bones are usually easy to remove after cooking, but this does mean disrupting the surface of the fish. So, for some dishes you'll want to take the bones out first.

To fillet a whole cleaned salmon or other large fish, start by cutting off the head and tail with a heavy, sharp knife. Insert the knife into the cavity at the head end, then cut the fish in half lengthwise, straight along the backbone. You'll be cutting down through a set of rib bones. Grasp the backbone of the fish at the head end and pull it out slowly, taking one set of rib bones out along with the spine. Then run the knife closely under the remaining set of rib bones and lift them out. Press the flesh with your fingertips to locate the remaining bones; you'll feel the tips of the bones like pinpricks. Pull them out with tweezers. The fish can then be cut into chunks so you can remove more small bones, or you can cook the sides whole.

To fillet a small fish such as a trout or a sardine, start with a cleaned fish with the head and skin on. Place the fish on a flat surface with the backbone facing you and the incision away from you. Using a sharp flexible knife with a thin blade, make a cut directly behind the head and push the knife straight down until you reach the backbone. Hold the knife in place against the backbone and turn the blade toward the tail of the fish. Start to cut away one fillet, keeping the knife against the backbone. Once the blade of the knife is completely under the fillet, place your hand flat on top of the fish and cut the rest of the fillet off the backbone, cutting through the rib bones. Keep the knife flat and as close to the backbone as possible. Lift the fillet off the backbone, turn the fish over and cut the fillet off the other side. Place the fillet skin side down and work the tip of the knife under the rib bones. Keeping the knife as close as possible to the ribs, slide the blade of the knife along the top of the fillet to cut the ribs off in one piece. Repeat with the other fillet. Check to see if there are pin bones remaining in the fish; these can be pulled out using tweezers or pliers.

If you want the fish in one piece, you can butterfly it using a sharp, flexible filleting knife with a thin blade. Use a big knife for larger fish, a smaller knife for little ones. Start with a cleaned fish with the skin on. Cut off the head and open the cavity of the fish, holding the fish at the head end. Place the tip of the knife at the head end along the side of the backbone and carefully work the knife down along the backbone to the tail end of the fish, cutting though the rib bones as you go. Repeat along the other side of the backbone; lift out the backbone and break it off at the tail end. Then put the tip of the filleting knife under the rib bones on one side of the fish and carefully cut out along the underside of the bones, keeping as close as possible to the rib bones as you go. Lift off the rib bones in a single piece and repeat on the other side of the fish. Check to see if there are pin bones remaining in the fish; these can be pulled out using tweezers or pliers.

Fish can be filleted before or after freezing. You will have to defrost a frozen fish before you can fillet it; always allow the fish to defrost in the refrigerator, which prevents bacterial growth. I prefer to thaw frozen fish before cooking it.

CLEANING AND PREPARING SHELLFISH

If you buy live oysters, clams, mussels, or scallops, wash them thoroughly under cold running water before you cook them. If the mussel has a little "beard" on it, snip it off with scissors; don't pull it off or you may kill the mussel. The shells should be shut tight until they are cooked, at which point they should open completely. Discard any oysters, mussels, clams, or scallops that do not open when they are cooked.

It's difficult to open clams or mussels without cooking them first, and for this reason they are generally cooked in the shell unless you are buying them already shucked. It's a little easier to shuck an oyster. Wear heavy gloves to do this, as it's easy to cut yourself with the knife or on the sharp edge of a shell. Use an oyster knife or a knife with a short, flat, sharp blade. Hold the shell at the narrow end, flat side down and with the opening to one side; insert the point of the knife between the two shells close to the middle of the oyster. Work the knife back and forth to loosen the shell. When the shell opens even slightly, slide the knife around the edge of the oyster and try to cut the adductor muscle that's holding it closed. Once you've got the shell open, slide the knife under the oyster to cut the muscle holding it onto the shell. The liquid inside the oyster is delicious and can be added to most recipes, especially soups and chowders.

It's most common to buy prawns that are not alive. Although some prawns are sold with the heads on, these are easy to remove. You should take the heads off before storing prawns in the fridge or freezer—otherwise the meat can turn mushy. Cut off the heads with a sharp knife or twist them off with your hand. To remove the shell of an uncooked prawn or shrimp, cut the shell up the back with a pair of thin, sharp scissors. Carefully peel off the shells, removing the legs at the front at the same time. The shells of spot prawns can be very sharp, so use caution when removing them. If there is an egg sac, it will come off easily with the shell. Sometimes there's a dark vein visible; it's actually the intestinal tract of the prawn, not a vein at all, and it often empties out entirely when the prawn trap is raised. The vein will not affect the flavour of the prawn. However, if it bothers you, pick out this dark bit with the point of a paring knife. If you're eating cold-water prawns, this step is generally not necessary.

You can freeze prawns and shrimp either before or after they are cooked. Make sure to place them in an airtight container so they don't develop freezer burn. Don't leave prawns or shrimp in the freezer for more than two months.

Preparing live crab or lobster requires special care so the animal does not suffer unduly. I prefer to clean crab before cooking it. First, I have to kill the crab. I do this by cutting into the crab with the point of a sharp knife, right between the eyes. Next I cut the body in half top to bottom and scrape out the intestines and lungs, which are light in colour and shaped like fronds. I discard these innards, which I don't want to eat, but the body does contain lots of good meat. After rinsing both halves under cold running water, I scrape the inside of the body cavity with the point of a knife to get out the last remaining bits of entrail. It's much easier to shell the crab after it's been cooked, so I put the cleaned crab into a big pot of simmering water and allow it to cook for twelve minutes. Then I take out the pieces, rinse them under cold water to stop the cooking, and drain the crab thoroughly. Crack the shells with a lobster cracker or a nutcracker, or just use a hammer. The meat can be picked out with a fork.

I cook lobster first and then clean it. Start with a large pot filled with salted water. Bring it to a boil, then add the lobsters. The boiling water will kill them quickly. Bring the water back to a boil on high heat and cook for five minutes per pound. Don't overcook the lobsters or they will become tough. Try pulling out one of the antennae; if it comes out easily, the lobster is cooked. Remove the lobsters with tongs, drain well, and allow them to cool slightly. Serve them whole and let people crack their own lobsters at the table, or cut the lobsters in half lengthwise with a large knife and remove the tail meat. Crack the claws and knuckles with a lobster cracker, a nutcracker, or a hammer, then pick out the meat with your fingers or with a lobster pick. Serve the meat on a platter or add it to your favourite recipe.

Cooked crab or lobster can be frozen, but eat it as soon as it begins to defrost. Cooked crab or lobster meat can be frozen in an airtight container for up to three months.

CLEANING AND PREPARING SQUID AND OCTOPUS

It's possible to buy whole squid or cleaned squid, either fresh or frozen. To clean squid, grasp the squid body at its tip with one hand and pull hard on the head and tentacles with the other. The head, the ink sac, and most of the guts will come out together. Try not to break the ink sac, as it can be quite messy. Then pull out the spine, cut into one wing, run your finger from its tip to the hood, and peel the skin and the other wing away like an orange rind. Then turn the mantle inside out to remove any remaining viscera. Cut the tentacles from the head just above the eyes and check to be sure the beak is not attached. (You can reserve the ink sac to make risotto or pasta, too. You should use it within twenty-four hours.)

Most octopus is sold cleaned, cut into large pieces, and frozen. If you buy frozen octopus, defrost it in the fridge for about twenty-four hours. You may choose to remove the suction cups (they can be chewy). It's easiest to do this after you've cooked the octopus; when it is cool, you can pull the suction cups off with your fingers. If you buy whole fresh octopus, and you find cleaning it a challenge, you can cut the webbing between the tentacles to the very top of the tentacles, then cut across the top of the tentacle to free it from the head. Repeat with the remaining tentacles and discard the head. Use the tentacles in the recipe.

Cooking Times for Fish and Seafood

SHRIMP AND PRAWNS

Shrimp and prawns cook very quickly, usually in about two minutes. They can be cooked with their shells on or off, and the shells won't affect the cooking time by more than a minute. When the colour of the shells, or of the flesh itself, lightens and becomes opaque, the shrimp are cooked. Also, the texture will change—the flesh becomes firmer as it cooks, so you can press it with your finger or a fork and judge it that way. Shrimp and prawns will continue to cook off the heat, and they are better undercooked than overcooked, so err on the side of caution.

OYSTERS

Oysters will cook very quickly. You are really just heating up the oyster, so it will only take a minute or two. The appearance won't change a lot, but when the edges of a raw oyster start to ruffle, the oyster is cooked. It will get a little firmer too. If you're cooking oysters in the shell, the oysters will open when they are cooked—this could take from five to ten minutes—and should be taken off the heat right away. Discard any oysters that fail to open.

CLAMS AND MUSSELS

Clams and mussels will become slightly firmer when they are cooked. Fresh clams and mussels are almost always sold in their shells; they are cooked when their shells open, which usually takes from five to ten minutes, depending on the heat. Discard any clams or mussels that fail to open. If you are using canned clams, they are generally already cooked and simply need to be heated through.

FISH

The best way to test if fish is cooked is to try to flake it with a fork. If it flakes, it's cooked, and this is true for any fish. Often the appearance of the flesh will provide a second clue: it will turn from translucent to opaque as it cooks. Fish is better undercooked than overcooked, so keep a close eye on it. And remember, it will continue to cook once it's off the heat, so take it off as soon as it flakes. A lean fish, such as trout, will dry out more easily than an oily fish, such as salmon, and requires extra vigilance.

Sometimes it's difficult to see if the flesh flakes. In this case, you can use an instant-read thermometer. When the heat measures 120°F at the thickest point, you can take it off the heat and allow it to finish cooking for a minute or two, until the thermometer reads 125 to 130°F. Having a thermometer is really useful when you're cooking a whole fish, or when the pieces of fish are in a sauce or wrapped in pastry that you don't want to cut.

BASIC COOKING TIMES FOR FISH

You can estimate the amount of time a piece of fish will take to cook by measuring it at its thickest part. The following table is a guideline to the amount of time you'll need for various cuts and cooking methods. These times are useful for planning your meal but are only approximate. You should also use your own judgement and test the fish as described above to know when it is done.

BASIC COOKING TIMES FOR FISH

NOTE: small fish take proportionally longer to cook than large fish

BAKING	TYPE OF FISH	TEMPERATURE	TIME
	whole fish	400°F	10 minutes per inch or 10 to 15 minutes per pound
	fillets, steaks, or chunks	350°F	10 minutes per inch

BROILING	TYPE OF FISH	TEMPERATURE	TIME
	whole small fish (1 to 2 lbs)	high, fish positioned about 2 inches from the broiler	5 minutes per side
	fillets, steaks, or chunks (½ to 1 inch thick)	high, fish positioned about 2 inches from the broiler	2 to 3 minutes per side
	fillets, steaks, or chunks (2 inches thick)	high, fish positioned about 2 inches from the broiler	4 minutes per side

GRILLING	TYPE OF FISH	TEMPERATURE	TIME
	whole fish (1 to 2 lbs)	high	3 to 5 minutes per side
	whole fish (5 to 6 lbs)	high	8 to 10 minutes per side
	fillets, steaks, or chunks (1 inch thick)	high	2 minutes per side
	fillets, steaks, or chunks (2 inches thick)	high	3 to 4 minutes per side

POACHING	TYPE OF FISH		TIME
	small whole fish or large chunks		6 to 8 minutes per pound
	fillets or steaks		5 to 10 minutes

Classic Fish Stock

CAMERON GREAVES, Stock Up, Vancouver

HALIBUT Atlantic, Pacific, Canada, bottom long-line: *some concerns;* US, trawled: *Avoid*

NOTE Fish stock can also be made using other types of fish bones or shellfish. For example, you can use lobster shells to make lobster stock, or combine several kinds of fish. Avoid using oily fish such as tuna or salmon.

Place fish bones, trimmings, and water in a large saucepan. Squeeze lemon juice into the water, then add squeezed lemon, onions, carrots, celery, peppercorns, parsley, bay leaf, and thyme. Heat to a simmer on medium-high heat, then allow to cook for 15 minutes, no longer. Remove from the heat.

Using a large spoon, skim the surface and discard any foamy residue. Strain stock through a fine-mesh sieve, discarding the solids. Use immediately or allow to cool. Will keep refrigerated in an airtight container for up to 3 days or frozen for up to 1 month.

Makes 2½ cups

1 lb halibut bones and lean trimmings, well rinsed

2½ cups cold water

½ lemon

1 onion, chopped

1 carrot, peeled and chopped

2 stalks celery with leaves, chopped

5 black peppercorns

2 sprigs Italian flat-leaf parsley, whole

1 bay leaf

Pinch of dried thyme

fish

Pan-roasted Arctic Char with Lobster Mashed Potatoes and Pinot Noir Sauce

MICHAEL HOWELL, Tempest Restaurant, Wolfville, Nova Scotia

ARCTIC CHAR *Best choice*

LOBSTER Atlantic Canada: *Best choice*; Atlantic US: *Some concerns*; Rock, spiny, US, Australia, Western Baja: *Best choice*; Spiny, international: *Avoid*

LOBSTER
MASHED POTATOES
4 large Russet or
Yukon Gold potatoes,
peeled and chopped

½ cup whipping
cream or milk,
warmed

¼ cup butter

¼ cup lobster stock
(page 21)

½ lb cooked
lobster meat

PINOT NOIR SAUCE
1 cup Pinot Noir

1 shallot, chopped

2 sprigs fresh
thyme, whole

1 cup fish stock
(page 21)

1 cup beef or
veal stock

2 Tbsp butter, cold

LOBSTER MASHED POTATOES In a large saucepan of salted water, boil potatoes on medium-high heat until tender, about 18 minutes.

Drain potatoes, return to the saucepan, and mash. Using a wooden spoon, stir in cream (or milk) and butter. Slowly stir in lobster stock, a few tablespoons at a time, until potatoes are smooth and fluffy. Gently fold in lobster meat. Cover and keep warm on low heat.

PINOT NOIR SAUCE In a medium saucepan on medium-high heat, gently boil red wine, shallot, and thyme until the liquid is reduced by half, 5 to 6 minutes. Add fish stock and gently boil until reduced by half, 5 to 6 minutes. Add beef (or veal) stock and gently boil until reduced by half once more, 5 to 6 minutes. Remove from the heat and discard thyme. Whisk in butter until fully incorporated and the sauce has a shine. Cover and keep warm on low heat.

PAN-ROASTED ARCTIC CHAR Preheat the oven to 350°F.

Heat butter and olive oil in a large cast-iron frying pan on medium-high heat. Add 3 of the fillets and fry until golden, about 3 minutes per side. Transfer pan-fried fillets to a baking sheet. Pan-fry the remaining 3 fillets, adding more olive oil if necessary, and transfer them to the baking sheet. Roast in the oven until just cooked through, about 4 minutes.

TO SERVE Spoon lobster mashed potatoes onto the centre of six plates. Top with a fillet of Arctic char and drizzle the plates with sauce.

Serves 6

PAN-ROASTED
ARCTIC CHAR
1 tsp butter

1 to 2 Tbsp olive oil

6 skinless Arctic
char fillets (each 5 oz)

Pan-fried Arctic Char with Whitefish Caviar and New Potato Salad

TERRY GERETA, Mise Restaurant, Winnipeg

ARCTIC CHAR *Best choice*

WHITEFISH *See Freshwater Fish, page 167*

16 small new potatoes, boiled, cooled, and cut in quarters

½ cup sour cream

1 Tbsp fresh dill, chopped

8 strips boar bacon or regular bacon, chopped

⅓ cup all-purpose flour

2 skinless Arctic char fillets (each 6 oz), cut in half crosswise

6 Tbsp whitefish caviar (also known as golden caviar) (optional)

1 Tbsp finely chopped pickled beets

In a bowl, gently toss potatoes with sour cream and dill. Season with salt and pepper. Set aside.

Line a plate with a paper bag. In a frying pan, sauté bacon on medium-high heat until crispy, about 5 minutes. Remove from the pan and transfer to the paper bag–lined plate to drain. Reserve the bacon fat.

Spread flour on a plate. Season both sides of Arctic char with salt and pepper, then dredge in the flour, shaking off any excess.

Reheat bacon fat in the frying pan on medium-high heat. When the fat is hot, add fillets and pan-fry on one side until golden, about 3 minutes. Turn fillets over and cook about 3 minutes more.

TO SERVE Arrange potato salad in the middle of each plate. Place a fillet atop each mound of salad. Spoon whitefish caviar around the base of the salad, then sprinkle with beets and bacon.

Serves 4

Almond-crusted Catfish Fillets

ANDREW CHASE, *Homemakers* magazine

CATFISH North American, farmed: *Best choice*;
International, farmed: *Some concerns*

In a shallow dish, whisk together flour, salt, cayenne, and black pepper. Place eggs in a second shallow dish, and almonds in a third. Dredge both sides of each catfish fillet in the flour mixture, then dip in egg. Dip fillets in almonds, pressing nuts lightly onto the fish until well coated.

Heat olive (or vegetable) oil in a frying pan on medium-high heat. Add catfish fillets and fry for 1½ to 2½ minutes. Turn fillets over and cook for 1½ to 2½ minutes more, or until the fish flakes easily. The almonds should be nicely browned when the fish is done. (If the frying pan is not big enough to hold all of the fillets, cook in batches, adding more oil as necessary to stop the fish from sticking.)

TO SERVE Arrange catfish fillets on four warmed plates. Sprinkle with sea salt to taste and serve with wedges of lemon.

Serves 4

2 Tbsp all-purpose flour

¼ tsp salt

¼ tsp cayenne pepper

¼ tsp black pepper

2 eggs, beaten

1½ cups finely chopped raw or blanched almonds

4 skinless catfish fillets (each 6 oz)

½ cup olive oil or vegetable oil

1 lemon, in 8 wedges, for garnish

Dogfish Ceviche in Five Elements

MARIO NAVARRETE JR., Raza, Montreal

DOGFISH Pacific: *Some concerns*; Atlantic: *Avoid*

HALIBUT Atlantic, Pacific, Canada, bottom long-line: *Some concerns*; US, trawled: *Avoid*

1 lb sashimi-grade dogfish or halibut fillets, in very thin strips

1 red onion, very finely sliced

¼ tsp rocoto paste or puréed chipotle peppers

¼ tsp salt

Juice of 8 limes

2 ice cubes

6 to 7 sprigs cilantro, for garnish

4 sweet potatoes, peeled and boiled

NOTE Rocoto paste is made from medium-hot red chili peppers and is available at Latin food markets.

Place dogfish or halibut in a medium bowl. Rinse red onions under cold running water and drain well, shaking off any remaining water. Add onions to the fish and toss gently to combine. Stir in rocoto paste (or puréed chipotle peppers) and salt. Add lime juice and toss the ceviche gently. Stir in ice cubes for 2 minutes to refresh the fish, removing them before they start to melt.

TO SERVE Divide ceviche among four plates and garnish each serving with cilantro. Serve immediately with boiled sweet potatoes.

Serves 4 as a first course

Champion Potato Seafood Chowder

DUNCAN SMITH, Claddagh Oyster House, Charlottetown

HADDOCK Canada, bottom long-line: *Best choice;*
US, bottom long-line: *Some concerns;* Trawled: *Avoid*

HALIBUT Atlantic, Pacific, Canada, bottom long-line: *Some concerns;*
US, trawled: *Avoid*

SALMON Pacific, wild: *Some concerns;* Farmed: *Avoid*

Melt butter in a large stockpot on medium-high heat. Add onions, celery, carrots, and red peppers. Sauté until tender, about 10 minutes. Add flour and stir to mix evenly. Cook, stirring constantly, for 5 minutes. Reduce the heat to medium-low. Gradually add lobster stock, stirring well between additions to prevent lumps. Increase the heat to medium-high and bring to a boil. Add potatoes, reduce the heat to medium, and cook until the potatoes are just tender, about 15 minutes. Keep warm on low heat.

In another stockpot, bring cream and orange liqueur just to a boil on medium-high heat. Reduce the heat to medium, add mixed fish, and simmer gently until almost completely cooked, about 5 minutes. (Mussels should be open; discard any that remain closed.)

Add the fish mixture to the soup, and season with salt and pepper. Stir in the chives.

TO SERVE Ladle chowder into eight warmed bowls, distributing the seafood evenly. Serve immediately. (Leftover chowder can be refrigerated in an airtight container for up to 24 hours, then reheated gently on medium-low heat.)

Serves 8

- 4 Tbsp butter
- 1 onion, diced
- ½ cup diced celery
- ½ cup diced carrots
- ½ cup diced red bell peppers
- 2 Tbsp all-purpose flour
- 2 cups lobster stock (page 21)
- 1 lb Russet potatoes, peeled and diced
- 8 cups half-and-half cream
- ¼ cup orange liqueur, such as Triple Sec
- 3 lbs mixed chowder fish, such as haddock, halibut, salmon, crab, lobster, mussels, and shucked oysters, in ½-inch dice
- ¼ cup finely chopped chives

Finnan Haddie and Chorizo Chowder

MICHAEL HOWELL, Tempest Restaurant, Wolfville, Nova Scotia

HADDOCK Canada, bottom long-line: *Best choice*;
US, bottom long-line: *Some concerns*; Trawled: *Avoid*

3 Tbsp good-
quality olive oil

1½ lbs chorizo sausage
(about 4 links), casings
removed and sausage
roughly chopped
in 1-inch dice

1 large carrot,
peeled and diced

2 stalks celery, diced

1 large white onion, diced

3 cloves garlic, minced

¼ tsp hot red pepper flakes

4 bay leaves

1 lb white potatoes,
peeled and diced

3 cans (each 14½ oz)
whole evaporated milk

2 cups fish stock
(page 21) or water

2 to 3 dashes Tabasco sauce

1 lb smoked line-caught
haddock, skin trimmed,
bones removed, and thin
tail pieces reserved for
stock (see note)

NOTE Make a flavourful smoked haddock stock
by adding the trimmings to regular fish stock
or water. Carrot peelings, onion and celery scraps,
and fresh thyme are also good additions. Simmer
for 1 hour, strain through a fine-mesh sieve,
then use in place of fish stock in this recipe.

In a large stockpot, heat olive oil on medium heat.
Add sausage and cook for 10 minutes, stirring to
break into small bits. When the sausage is mostly
cooked but not crispy, add carrots, celery, and
onions and cook for another 10 minutes.

Stir in garlic, red pepper flakes, bay leaves,
potatoes, evaporated milk, and fish stock (or
water). Season with Tabasco and salt and pepper
and bring to a simmer, stirring occasionally to
prevent the chowder from sticking to the bottom
of the pot. (Be careful not to boil or the evaporated milk will split; this won't affect the flavour
but it will affect the look of the dish.)

Once the chowder is simmering, cook for
10 minutes or until the potatoes are mostly
cooked. Add haddock and cook gently until the
fish flakes, about 10 minutes. Season to taste
with more salt and pepper. Remove from the heat.
For best results, refrigerate the soup overnight
to allow the flavours to infuse.

Just before serving, gently reheat the soup
on medium-low heat for 8 to 10 minutes.

TO SERVE Ladle the chowder into individual
warmed bowls and enjoy.

Serves 6

Pan-seared Haddock with Seasonal Salad and Yellow Tomato Vinaigrette

RENÉE LAVALLÉE, The Five Fishermen, Halifax

HADDOCK Canada, bottom long-line: *Best choice*;
US, bottom long-line: *Some concerns*; Trawled: *Avoid*

YELLOW TOMATO VINAIGRETTE In a blender, process tomatoes, olive oil, champagne (or white wine) vinegar, and pinches of salt and ground pepper until smooth. Will keep refrigerated in an airtight container for 1 week.

SALAD Fry prosciutto in a frying pan on medium-high heat until crisp, about 5 minutes, then set aside to cool.

Crumble 3 slices of the prosciutto into a bowl. Add cress, radishes, and apple and toss until well combined.

PAN-SEARED HADDOCK Heat olive oil in a large frying pan on high heat. Season haddock fillets with salt and ground pepper. Place fillets, skin side up, in the pan and cook for 4 minutes. Turn the fillets over and cook until the fish feels firm to the touch, 2 to 4 more minutes.

TO SERVE In a small bowl, toss the salad with a tablespoon of the vinaigrette. Divide the salad among six plates and top with a haddock fillet. Drizzle the plates with the remaining vinaigrette and crumble the remaining prosciutto over the top.

Serves 6

YELLOW TOMATO VINAIGRETTE
3 yellow tomatoes, chopped

¼ cup extra-virgin olive oil

2 Tbsp champagne vinegar or white wine vinegar

SALAD
6 slices prosciutto

1 cup upland cress or watercress

6 radishes, thinly sliced

1 Granny Smith apple, unpeeled, cored and julienned

PAN-SEARED HADDOCK
1 Tbsp extra-virgin olive oil

6 haddock fillets (each 6 oz), skin on

Pan-fried Haddock with Fresh Herbs and Brown Butter

JOEL ROUSELL, Saege Bistro, Halifax

HADDOCK Canada, bottom long-line: *Best choice*; US, bottom long-line: *Some concerns*; Trawled: *Avoid*

1 lb fingerling potatoes, scrubbed and cut in half lengthwise

¼ cup olive oil

12 baby carrots, cleaned and blanched

6 Tbsp unsalted butter

4 haddock fillets (each 5 oz), skin on

1 Tbsp fresh dill, finely chopped

1 Tbsp fresh Italian flat-leaf or curly-leaf parsley, finely chopped

1 Tbsp fresh tarragon, finely chopped

12 baby zucchini, cleaned and blanched

Preheat the oven to 400°F. Line a baking sheet with parchment paper.

In a small bowl, toss potatoes with 1 to 2 Tbsp of the olive oil (just enough to coat). Season with fine sea salt and freshly cracked pepper. Transfer to the baking sheet and cook in the oven for about 40 minutes, or until potatoes are golden.

In a second small bowl, toss carrots with 2 tsp of the olive oil. Season with fine sea salt and freshly cracked pepper. Arrange carrots in an ovenproof baking dish, dab with 1 Tbsp of the butter, and bake for about 20 minutes, or until golden. (You can roast the potatoes and carrots at the same time.)

Place haddock on a plate and evenly sprinkle both sides of each fillet with salt and pepper.

Heat a frying pan on medium-high heat. Add 2 Tbsp of the butter, and when it is sizzling, add haddock, skin side up. Gently shake the pan to ensure the fish does not stick. Cook for about 3 minutes, or until the fish has browned nicely. Turn haddock over, adding another 2 Tbsp of butter and the dill, parsley, and tarragon. Reduce the heat to medium. Shake the pan gently and continue to pan-fry haddock until cooked through, 5 to 8 minutes. When the fillets are done, the butter should be light brown and have a nutty caramel flavour. Remove from the heat and set aside.

Just before serving, place zucchini and the remaining butter in a frying pan on high heat. Season with salt and pepper and cook until warmed through.

TO SERVE Place a haddock fillet on each of four warmed plates. Divide the carrots and potatoes evenly around the fish. Top with zucchini, drizzle with the brown butter and serve warm.

Serves 4

Crispy Hake in Curried Mussel Stew

STELIO PEROMBELON, Les ConsServent, Montreal

HAKE Pacific: *Best choice*

MUSSELS Farmed: *Best choice*; Wild: *Some concerns*

CURRIED MUSSEL STEW

2 tsp olive oil

1 tsp minced shallots

1 tsp Indian curry powder

1 lb mussels, cleaned and beards snipped off

½ cup water

½ cup white wine

¼ cup whipping cream

16 slender asparagus spears, trimmed

10 basil leaves

½ bulb fennel, cored and thinly sliced

½ cup cooked fava beans

1 tsp chopped chives

2 Tbsp butter

CURRIED MUSSEL STEW Heat olive oil in a large saucepan on medium heat. Add shallots, stirring often until translucent, about 3 minutes. Add curry powder and stir for 3 minutes or until fragrant, then add mussels, water, and white wine. Cover and cook until mussels open, 4 to 6 minutes. Discard any mussels that don't open. Using a slotted spoon, transfer the mussels to a plate, reserving the cooking liquid. Remove mussels from their shells and set aside. Discard the shells.

Strain the cooking liquid through a fine-mesh sieve into an ovenproof frying pan just large enough to hold the hake. Set the pan on medium-high heat and bring to a boil. Cook, stirring often, until the liquid is reduced by half, about 8 minutes. Add cream and boil for 1 minute. Remove from the heat and stir in asparagus, basil leaves, fennel, and fava beans. Cover and set aside.

CRISPY HAKE Preheat the oven to 350°F.

Place panko in a small shallow dish. Heat olive oil in a large cast-iron frying pan on medium-high heat. Season hake with salt and pepper, then dredge just one side of each fillet in panko. Pan-fry hake, coated side down, until bread crumbs are golden, 2 to 3 minutes.

Add hake fillets to the pan of asparagus and fava beans, coated side up. Bake until the hake is cooked through, 8 to 10 minutes. Using a slotted spoon, transfer the fillets to a plate.

FINISH STEW Add chives, mussels, and butter to the pan of stew. Heat on low heat until butter melts completely. Stir well to combine.

TO SERVE Ladle curried mussel stew into individual bowls. Top each serving with a piece of crispy hake and garnish with cilantro leaves.

Serves 4

CRISPY HAKE

3/4 cup panko
(Japanese bread crumbs)

1/4 cup olive oil

4 skinless hake fillets
(each 4 to 6 oz)

2 Tbsp organic baby
cilantro leaves

Duck Bacon–wrapped Halibut Cheeks with Tomato Fennel Sauce

MATTHEW HORN, The Masthead Restaurant,
Cowichan Bay, British Columbia

HALIBUT Atlantic, Pacific, Canada, bottom long-line: *Some concerns*;
US, trawled: *Avoid*

SMOKED DUCK BACON
½ cup canola oil

2 Tbsp soy sauce

2 Tbsp Worcestershire sauce

1 Tbsp grainy mustard

¼ cup maple syrup

1 tsp ground black pepper

1 duck breast (12 oz or larger), skin on, boneless

mesquite wood chips

2 ripe tomatoes, in half

TOMATO FENNEL SAUCE
2 Tbsp canola oil

1 bulb fennel, roughly chopped

1 onion, roughly chopped

1 large carrot, peeled and roughly chopped

1 stalk celery, roughly chopped

3 cloves garlic, roughly chopped

¼ cup white wine

3 Tbsp butter

NOTE This dish can also be made using store-bought prosciutto as a substitute for the duck bacon. You will need 8 to 12 slices of prosciutto cut into strips, one for each piece of halibut cheek. (If you use prosciutto, you won't need the marinade.) Roast the tomatoes in a 400°F oven for 10 minutes before adding them to the sauce.

SMOKED DUCK BACON In a bowl large enough to hold the duck breast, combine canola oil, soy sauce, Worcestershire sauce, grainy mustard, maple syrup, and pepper. Add duck breast, being sure to coat it well with the marinade. Cover and refrigerate for 24 hours.

Place mesquite wood chips in a wood smoker or a barbecue. Preheat until the wood chips start to smoke.

Rinse the duck breast under cold running water, then pat dry with a clean tea towel. Place duck breast and tomatoes in the smoker (or barbecue) for 1½ hours. (The smoked duck will still be raw.) Remove duck breast and tomatoes from the heat and allow to cool. Slice duck breast lengthwise as thinly as possible. You will need one slice for each piece of halibut cheek.

TOMATO FENNEL SAUCE Heat canola oil in a frying pan on medium-high heat. Add fennel, onions, carrots, celery, and garlic and sauté for 3 to 5 minutes, or until onions are translucent. Add white wine, stirring to deglaze the pan, then cook until wine is reduced to a teaspoon. Stir in smoked tomatoes and add just enough water to cover.

Bring the sauce to a boil, then simmer for 10 minutes. Remove from the heat and allow to cool.

Purée the sauce in a food processor or with a hand blender until it is smooth. Set aside.

HALIBUT CHEEKS Preheat the oven to 350°F.

Lay a strip of duck bacon, one end toward you, on a clean work surface. Place a piece of halibut cheek on the end and roll the bacon away from you, completely encasing the halibut in the bacon. Press a toothpick through the bacon and into the halibut to secure the end. Repeat with the remaining bacon slices and halibut pieces. Season with salt and pepper.

Heat an ovenproof stainless steel frying pan on medium-high heat, then add butter and canola oil. Once the pan is sizzling, sear wrapped halibut pieces on one side until the bacon is caramelized, about 3 minutes. Transfer to the oven and cook for 2 to 3 minutes, or until the halibut is flaky but not dry in the centre. Remove from the oven.

FINISH SAUCE Heat sauce in a medium saucepan on medium heat. Stir in butter until well combined.

TO SERVE Spoon two tablespoons of the sauce onto each plate. Divide the bacon-wrapped halibut cheeks (two to three per serving) evenly among the plates, then garnish with chopped rosemary and thyme.

Serves 4 as a first course

HALIBUT CHEEKS
1 lb halibut cheeks, in 1½-inch dice

1 Tbsp butter

1 Tbsp canola oil

1 Tbsp freshly chopped rosemary, for garnish

1 Tbsp freshly chopped thyme, for garnish

Halibut with Tomato, Basil, and Garlic Sauce

SUSAN MENDELSON, The Lazy Gourmet, Vancouver

HALIBUT Atlantic, Pacific, Canada, bottom long-line: *Some concerns;* US, trawled: *Avoid*

1 can (28 oz) whole tomatoes, including juice

4 cups basil leaves, finely chopped

½ cup vegetable stock

6 skinless halibut fillets (each 6 oz)

2 Tbsp white wine

3 large cloves garlic, minced

Preheat the oven to 425°F. Lightly oil a 9 × 13-inch glass baking dish. Cut a 9 × 13-inch sheet of parchment paper and lightly spray one side with oil. Set aside.

Chop tomatoes in a food processor or blender, then transfer to a large saucepan on medium-high heat. Bring to a boil, stirring often, and cook until thickened, 5 to 7 minutes. Add basil and season with salt and pepper. Remove from the heat and set aside.

In another saucepan, on high heat, bring vegetable stock to a boil.

Arrange halibut in a single layer in the glass baking dish and drizzle with white wine. Pour the boiling vegetable stock over the fillets. Cover with the parchment paper, oiled side down.

Bake halibut until it feels firm to the touch, about 12 minutes. Using a slotted spoon, carefully transfer the fillets to a plate. Cover with a piece of parchment paper to keep warm.

Pour the halibut cooking liquid into the tomato sauce and stir to combine. Add garlic and boil on medium-high heat until the sauce is thick, 5 to 7 minutes.

TO SERVE Arrange halibut fillets on individual plates. Ladle the sauce over the fish and serve immediately.

Serves 6

Line-caught Atlantic Halibut with Roasted Parsnips, Fresh Fiddleheads, and Kale

MONICA BAUCHÉ and DENNIS JOHNSTON, Fid Restaurant, Halifax

HALIBUT Atlantic, Pacific, Canada, bottom long-line: *Some concerns*; US, trawled: *Avoid*

VEGETABLES Separate kale into leaves and cut out the tough stems. Discard the stems and the tough outer leaves. Place in a steamer and set aside.

Melt 1 Tbsp of the butter in a medium frying pan (or saucepan) on low heat. Add parsnips and cook slowly until tender, about 15 minutes. Season with salt and pepper, then place in a low oven to keep warm.

SEARED HALIBUT Season halibut fillets with salt and pepper.

Generously coat a large frying pan with olive oil and set on medium-high heat. When the oil is fairly hot, place the fillets in the pan. Cook until the fish is golden brown and almost cooked through, about 5 minutes. Turn halibut over and cook until the fish is cooked through, about 2 minutes.

FINISH VEGETABLES While the halibut is cooking, bring water to a boil in the steamer.

Melt 2 Tbsp of the butter in a small saucepan on low heat and keep it warm.

Steam the kale for 3 minutes, then divide it among four plates and drizzle it with the melted butter.

In another frying pan, melt the remaining butter on medium heat. Add the fiddleheads and sauté until lightly browned and tender, 2 to 3 minutes.

TO SERVE Arrange a few parsnips and fiddleheads around the kale on each plate. Top with a halibut fillet. Serve immediately.

Serves 4

VEGETABLES
1 head of Russian kale or regular kale

4 Tbsp butter

6 to 8 winter parsnips, scrubbed and cut in thin sticks

1 lb fiddleheads, washed and scales removed

SEARED HALIBUT
4 skinless halibut fillets (each 6 oz)

2 Tbsp virgin olive oil

Baked Pacific Halibut with Herb Pesto and Warm Spring Vegetable Salad

LYNN CRAWFORD, Four Seasons Hotel, New York

HALIBUT Atlantic, Pacific, Canada, bottom long-line: *Some concerns*; US, trawled: *Avoid*

HERB PESTO
¼ cup chopped fresh dill

¼ cup chopped fresh Italian parsley

¼ cup chopped fresh mint

3 Tbsp capers

2 cloves garlic, minced

8 small anchovy fillets, minced

1 Tbsp Dijon mustard

¼ cup olive oil

2 Tbsp fresh lemon juice

SPRING VEGETABLE SALAD
½ tsp salt

12 baby carrots, cut in half lengthwise

1 bunch asparagus, peeled, in 1-inch pieces

1 cup green beans, trimmed

1 cup fingerling potatoes

2 Tbsp olive oil

1 Tbsp butter

2 shallots, finely diced

½ cup chanterelle mushrooms, cleaned, destemmed, and sliced

1 bunch chives, finely chopped

Zest of 1 lemon

HERB PESTO In a blender or a food processor, combine dill, parsley, mint, capers, garlic, anchovies, and Dijon mustard until mixed. With the motor running on high, add olive oil and lemon juice in a slow continuous stream until the pesto is well combined. Transfer to a small bowl and set aside. Will keep refrigerated in an airtight container for 2 to 3 days.

SPRING VEGETABLE SALAD Fill a medium saucepan three-quarters full with water. Stir in salt, then bring to a boil on high heat. Add carrots and cook for 2 minutes. Using a slotted spoon, transfer carrots to a colander and run cold water over them to stop the cooking. Drain and set aside.

Bring the water back to a boil, add asparagus and cook for 1 minute. Using a slotted spoon, transfer asparagus to a colander and run cold water over them to stop the cooking. Drain and set aside. Repeat with green beans, cooking them for 2 minutes. Discard the cooking water.

Fill the saucepan three-quarters full with water. Add potatoes and boil on medium-high heat until fork tender, 10 to 12 minutes. Allow to cool slightly, then cut in ½-inch thick rounds. Set aside.

BAKED HALIBUT Preheat the oven to 350°F.

Season halibut on both sides with salt and pepper. Coat a frying pan with olive oil and heat on medium-high heat. Add fillets and sear on one side for 2 minutes, or until golden. Turn halibut over and sear for another minute. Transfer fillets to a baking sheet and bake in the oven until cooked through, 3 to 5 minutes.

FINISH VEGETABLES While the halibut is cooking, heat olive oil and butter in a large frying pan on medium-high heat. Add shallots and mushrooms and cook for 2 to 3 minutes. Stir in carrots, asparagus, green beans, and potatoes. Season with salt and pepper and toss to mix evenly. When the vegetables are heated through, sprinkle with chives and lemon zest.

TO SERVE Divide warm vegetables among four plates. Top with halibut and drizzle with herb pesto. Garnish with fresh pea greens, if you wish.

Serves 4

BAKED HALIBUT

4 skinless halibut fillets (each 6 oz)

2 Tbsp olive oil

4 to 6 oz fresh pea greens, for garnish

Grilled Pacific Halibut with Charred Jalapeño–Honey Vinaigrette

TOM DOUGLAS, Etta's, Seattle

HALIBUT Atlantic, Pacific, Canada, bottom long-line: *Some concerns*; US, trawled: *Avoid*

JALAPEÑO-HONEY VINAIGRETTE

2 Tbsp minced shallots

2 Tbsp apple cider vinegar

1/2 tsp kosher salt

1 Tbsp honey

1 Tbsp chopped cilantro

1/2 tsp Dijon mustard

1/2 tsp minced garlic

1/4 cup + 1 tsp olive oil

1 red jalapeño pepper

GRILLED HALIBUT

4 skinless Pacific halibut fillets (each 6 oz)

2 to 3 Tbsp olive oil

JALAPEÑO-HONEY VINAIGRETTE In a bowl, combine shallots, cider vinegar, and kosher salt and allow to stand for 10 minutes.

Whisk in honey, cilantro, Dijon mustard, garlic, and the ¼ cup olive oil. Season to taste with freshly ground black pepper and kosher salt.

Heat the remaining olive oil in a small saucepan on high heat. When the oil is hot, add jalapeño and cook, turning often, until charred and blistered on all sides, about 2 minutes. Remove from the heat and set aside to cool.

Using a sharp knife, peel off the charred skin and cut off the core end. Cut jalapeño in half, then scrape out and discard the seeds. Finely chop jalapeño and add to the vinaigrette, whisking gently to combine.

GRILLED HALIBUT Preheat a charcoal barbecue to medium-high. Lightly brush halibut on both sides with olive oil and season with kosher salt and freshly ground black pepper.

Fold a clean cloth, lightly dip it in olive oil, and lightly brush the hot grilling rack, using tongs or oven mitts, if necessary. Place halibut directly on the oiled rack and grill 3 to 4 minutes. Turn halibut over and grill for another 3 to 4 minutes, until just cooked through.

TO SERVE Place one piece of halibut on each plate. Whisk the vinaigrette, then spoon over each serving.

Serves 4

Halibut with Stewed Carrots and Horseradish

VITALY PALEY, Paley's Place, Portland, Oregon

HALIBUT Atlantic, Pacific, Canada, bottom long-line: *Some concerns*; US, trawled: *Avoid*

NOTE This dish can be served warm but tastes great cold, after marinating for two to three hours. Leftovers taste even better the next day.

HORSERADISH Finely grate the horseradish. In a small bowl, combine horseradish, vinegar, sugar, and salt. Refrigerate, uncovered, for 12 hours. (If covered, the horseradish will develop a bitter taste.)

PAN-FRIED HALIBUT In a large, straight-sided frying pan, heat ½ cup of the vegetable oil on low heat. Stir in carrots and onions. Cook, covered but stirring occasionally, until the vegetables are soft, about 30 minutes.

Add ketchup, tomato paste, and sugar and cook for 10 minutes, stirring occasionally. Season with salt and freshly ground black pepper, and set aside.

Place the flour in a shallow dish. Season it with salt and freshly ground black pepper.

Line a large cutting board with paper towels. Heat the remaining vegetable oil in another large frying pan on medium heat. Dredge the halibut fillets in the flour, shaking off any excess. Brown on one side for 3 to 5 minutes. Turn the fillets over and brown for another 3 to 5 minutes. (If the frying pan is not big enough to hold all of the halibut, cook the fillets in batches, adding more oil as necessary to stop the fish from sticking.) Transfer the halibut to the board to drain.

TO SERVE Arrange the halibut fillets on a large serving platter. Cover evenly with the carrot mixture and serve with a bowl of horseradish on the side.

Serves 8

HORSERADISH

1 large piece fresh horseradish root (6 to 8 oz), peeled

1 cup distilled white vinegar

1 Tbsp granulated sugar

1 Tbsp salt

PAN-FRIED HALIBUT

¾ cup vegetable oil

5 large carrots, peeled and cut in ⅛-inch rounds

1 large yellow onion, finely chopped

¼ cup ketchup

1 Tbsp tomato paste

½ tsp granulated sugar

1 cup sifted all-purpose flour

8 skinless halibut fillets (each 4 to 5 oz)

Marinated Herring with Warm Apple and Potato Salad

JAMIE KENNEDY, Jamie Kennedy Kitchens, Toronto

HERRING *Best choice*

MARINATED HERRING
4 fresh herring fillets
(each 4 to 5 oz), skin on

¼ cup coarse sea salt

1 cup sweet apple cider

¼ cup apple cider vinegar

¼ cup finely diced shallots

APPLE AND POTATO SALAD
5 whole potatoes, unpeeled

1 apple, peeled, cored, and diced

1 onion, thinly sliced

2 Tbsp Dijon mustard

2 dill pickles, julienned

2 Tbsp dill pickle juice

¼ cup chopped fresh Italian flat-leaf parsley

1 Tbsp chopped fresh thyme

2 Tbsp sunflower or vegetable oil

MARINATED HERRING Place herring fillets, skin side down, on a ceramic plate. Season with sea salt. Loosely cover and refrigerate for 6 hours.

About an hour before serving, simmer apple cider in a small saucepan on medium heat, stirring often, until reduced to a syrup, 10 to 12 minutes. (Be especially careful toward the end of the cooking time not to allow the cider to burn or caramelize). Pour the apple syrup into a bowl, then stir in cider vinegar and shallots.

Rinse salted herring under cold running water, then place on a clean tea towel to dry. Arrange fillets, skin side down, in a single layer in the bottom of a ceramic dish. Spoon the shallot mixture over the herring and season with freshly ground black pepper. Allow to stand at room temperature while you prepare the salad.

APPLE AND POTATO SALAD Place potatoes in a pot of salted water and boil on medium heat until tender, 10 to 12 minutes. Drain and allow to cool for 10 minutes.

In a large bowl, combine apple, onions, Dijon mustard, pickles, pickle juice, parsley, thyme, and sunflower (or vegetable) oil. Season with salt and freshly ground black pepper.

Using a sharp knife, peel potatoes (they should still be a little warm). Discard the skins and slice potatoes into ⅓-inch rounds. Add potatoes to the apple mixture and toss until well combined.

TO SERVE Divide the salad among four plates. Drape a herring fillet over each serving, then spoon some of the shallot mixture over the salad.

Serves 4

Broiled Mackerel Fillets

ANDREW CHASE, *Homemakers* magazine

MACKEREL *Best choice*

Preheat the broiler to high. Lightly grease a broiler pan.

In a small bowl, stir together onions, parsley, olive (or canola) oil, and paprika. Season with salt and pepper. Using a spoon, spread this mixture over both sides of the mackerel fillets. Place mackerel, skin side down, on the broiler pan. Cook, without turning, for 4 to 6 minutes, or until the fish flakes easily. Remove from the oven.

TO SERVE Arrange mackerel fillets on individual plates. Serve warm with wedges of lemon.

Serves 4

2 Tbsp finely chopped green onions, white and green parts

2 Tbsp finely chopped fresh Italian flat-leaf parsley

4 tsp olive oil or canola oil

1 tsp paprika

2 fresh mackerels (each about 1¼ lbs), filleted, skin on

1 lemon, in 4 to 8 wedges, for garnish

Fillet of Lingcod with Littleneck Clam Vinaigrette

DAVID HAWKSWORTH, Vancouver

LINGCOD *Some concerns*

CLAMS Farmed: *Best choice*; Atlantic, soft shell: *Some concerns*; Atlantic, dredged: *Avoid*

LEMON DRESSING
Zest of 1 lemon

Juice of 2 lemons

⅓ cup extra-virgin olive oil

1 tsp granulated sugar

SEARED LINGCOD AND VINAIGRETTE
⅛ cup extra-virgin olive oil

4 lingcod fillets (each 5 oz), skin on

1 slice smoked bacon

20 littleneck clams

1 clove garlic, thinly sliced

⅓ cup white wine

⅓ cup fish stock (page 21)

¼ cup unsalted butter

1 Tbsp finely chopped chives

Pinch of cayenne pepper

Juice of ½ lemon

1 bulb fennel, shaved into thin slices

⅛ cup lemon dressing

LEMON DRESSING In a small bowl, mix all ingredients together and add kosher salt and freshly ground white pepper to taste. Combine until sugar is dissolved and the mixture is emulsified. Will keep refrigerated in an airtight container for 2 days.

SEARED LINGCOD AND VINAIGRETTE In a large frying pan, heat olive oil on high heat. Add lingcod, skin side down, and sear for 2 to 3 minutes until golden brown. Transfer the fillets to a plate.

Add bacon, clams, and garlic to the frying pan and sauté for 1 minute. Deglaze the pan with white wine and cook until the liquid is reduced by half, about 3 minutes. Using a slotted spoon, transfer the clams to a plate and set aside. Discard any clams that do not open.

Add fish stock to the pan and bring to a simmer on medium heat. Add fillets, skin side up, and cook until the liquid is reduced by half, about 4 minutes. Transfer the lingcod to a platter and discard the bacon.

Return the clams to the pan and whisk in butter, chives, cayenne, and lemon juice. Cook until butter is emulsified, about 2 minutes.

In a small bowl, toss fennel with lemon dressing.

TO SERVE Place a fillet in the middle of each of the plates. Spoon the clams and sauce around the lingcod and finish with the shaved fennel. Serve immediately.

Serves 4

Maple-Sake Marinated Northern Pike

BEN KRAMER, Dandelion Eatery, Winnipeg

NORTHERN PIKE *See Freshwater Fish, page 167*

NOTE Northern pike, or jackfish, has a row of large, Y-shaped bones. Don't try to pull these when the fish is raw or you will shred the fish. Ask your fishmonger to debone the fish for you.

MARINATED PIKE Place northern pike in a large shallow pan. In a small bowl, combine sake and maple syrup, then pour over the fillets. Cover with parchment paper and refrigerate for 2 hours.

Preheat the oven to 350°F. Drain fillets, discarding marinade, and pat dry. Heat grapeseed oil in a large frying pan on medium heat. When hot, add pike in a single layer. Cook just until lightly browned on both sides, 2 to 3 minutes per side. (If needed, cook them in batches, adding more oil to stop the fish from sticking.) Reserving the frying pan, transfer fillets to a baking sheet and roast until cooked through, 3 to 5 more minutes.

BELL PEPPER AND LEEK SAUCE In the frying pan used to cook the fish, melt butter on medium heat. Add yellow and red peppers and leeks and sauté on medium heat until tender, 4 to 5 minutes. Stir in white wine, deglazing the pan. When the wine is reduced by two-thirds, about 4 minutes, add fish stock and maple syrup. Bring to a boil, stirring often, until reduced by a quarter, about 5 minutes. Season with salt and pepper.

TO SERVE Place northern pike fillets on six plates and top with the bell pepper and leek sauce. (Serve with brown basmati rice and your favourite vegetables, or over a lightly dressed salad.)

Serves 6

MARINATED PIKE
6 skinless northern pike fillets (each 8 oz), deboned

1 cup sake (Japanese rice wine)

2/3 cup maple syrup

1 to 2 Tbsp grapeseed oil

BELL PEPPER AND LEEK SAUCE
1 Tbsp butter

1 yellow bell pepper, sliced

1 red bell pepper, sliced

1 leek, diced

1/3 cup white wine

1 1/2 cups fish stock (page 21)

1 Tbsp maple syrup

Northern Pike Poached in Canola Oil

JENNIFER COCKRALL-KING, *The Edible Prairie Journal*, Edmonton

NORTHERN PIKE *See Freshwater Fish, page 167*

TARTAR SAUCE
¼ cup minced shallots

¼ cup sweet pickles,
such as gherkins, minced

¼ cup minced pimentos
or red bell peppers

¼ cup capers, minced

2 Tbsp Dijon mustard

1 Tbsp fresh lemon juice

1 cup mayonnaise

OIL-POACHED
NORTHERN PIKE

4 cups canola oil, or more

3 to 4 sprigs fresh herbs,
whole, or 2 Tbsp dried
herbs, such as tarragon,
thyme, rosemary, or
marjoram

4 skinless northern pike
fillets (each 5 oz), bone-in

4 handfuls baby lettuces
and microgreens, washed,
dried, and torn in pieces

1 Tbsp chopped fresh
Italian flat-leaf parsley,
for garnish

NOTE Northern pike, or jackfish, has a row of large, Y-shaped bones sticking up through the fillet. Don't try to pull these when the fish is raw or you will end up shred fillet. Also, feel free to experiment with other flavourings such as a bit of garlic, hot chili flakes, or your favourite spice blend to make an aromatic infused oil for your fish.

TARTAR SAUCE In a small bowl, combine shallots, sweet pickles, pimentos (or red peppers), capers, Dijon mustard, lemon juice, and mayonnaise. Season to taste with salt and pepper. Will keep refrigerated in an airtight container for up to 1 week.

OIL-POACHED NORTHERN PIKE Preheat the oven to 200°F.

Pour canola oil into a wide-bottomed, straight-sided saucepan (we use a 10-inch round saucepan with 2¾-inch sides). Gently crush the leaves and stems of the fresh herbs to release more flavour, then add them to the pan.

Heat canola oil and herbs on low heat. Once the temperature reaches 150°F, small champagne-like bubbles will start to form on the fresh herbs, and the oil will begin to move around in ripples and rivers on the bottom of the pan. Continue heating the oil until it reaches 160°F to 180°F; you can check with a deep-frying thermometer to be sure you have the right temperature. Be very careful with the hot oil, though at this temperature it should not bubble too much.

Line a plate with a paper bag. Using tongs,
gently add two fillets to the saucepan, one at a
time, submerging them in the oil and being
careful not to overcrowd the pan. (Overcrowding
causes the oil temperature to drop too low.) Poach
for about 5 minutes, or until a fork penetrates the
fish easily. Transfer the cooked pike to the paper
bag–lined plate to drain, then keep warm in
the oven while you cook the remaining fillets.

TO SERVE Arrange a handful of salad greens
on each plate. Top with a piece of warm
northern pike and season with salt and pepper.
Add a dollop of tartar sauce and sprinkle
with parsley. Serve immediately.

Serves 4

Pan-fried Yellow Perch with Lemon Aioli

MICHAEL SULLIVAN, Merrill Inn, Picton, Ontario

LAKE PERCH *See Freshwater Fish, page 167*

LEMON AIOLI
2 egg yolks

1 clove garlic

¾ cup virgin olive oil

¼ cup canola oil

Juice of 2 lemons

PAN-FRIED YELLOW PERCH
1 cup all-purpose flour

2 Tbsp paprika

1 tsp garlic powder

2 tsp salt

2 tsp pepper

4 perch fillets
(each 8 oz), skin
on, deboned

¼ cup canola oil

2 Tbsp butter

2 Tbsp chopped
fresh dill, for garnish

LEMON AIOLI In a food processor, purée egg yolks and garlic until smooth, 2 to 3 minutes.

Whisk together olive and canola oils in a measuring cup. With the food processor running, very slowly drizzle ¾ cup of the mixed oils into the egg and garlic mixture. Process until the oil is emulsified and the mixture thickens, about 5 minutes. Add ½ of the lemon juice and process to combine. Slowly add the remaining mixed oils, alternating with the remaining lemon juice, until the aioli is thick and the ingredients are well mixed. Season with salt and pepper to taste. Will keep refrigerated in an airtight container for 24 hours.

PAN-FRIED YELLOW PERCH In a large shallow dish, combine flour, paprika, garlic powder, salt, and pepper, stirring gently until well mixed.

One at a time, dredge perch fillets in the flour mixture, coating them completely. Shake off any excess. Place the coated fillets on a large plate. Discard the leftover flour mixture.

Pour canola oil into a frying pan on high heat. When the oil just begins to smoke, carefully add perch fillets, skin side down. Dot butter evenly among the fillets and sauté for 3 minutes. Turn fillets over and cook another 30 seconds, or until fish flakes with a fork.

TO SERVE Place a perch fillet on each warmed plate, top with a generous dollop of the lemon aioli, and sprinkle with dill. Serve immediately.

Serves 4

Pickerel Tempura with Wasabi-Ginger Tartar Sauce

RÉMI COUSYN, Calories Bakery & Restaurant, Saskatoon

PICKEREL See Freshwater Fish, *page 167*

WASABI-GINGER TARTAR SAUCE In a bowl, combine mayonnaise, lemon juice, gherkins, capers, ginger, and wasabi powder. Stir in the pickled ginger juice. Set aside. Will keep refrigerated in an airtight container for up to 2 days.

PICKEREL TEMPURA Whisk egg yolks with water in a small bowl. In another small bowl, combine flour and cornstarch. Slowly add to the egg and water mixture, whisking constantly so the batter does not form lumps. Season with pinches of salt and pepper, then stir until well combined.

Line a large plate with a paper bag. In a large straight-sided frying pan, heat vegetable oil on medium-high heat to 360°F (use a deep-frying thermometer to check the temperature), or use a deep fryer if you have one.

Pat pickerel fillets dry with a tea towel. Working one fillet at a time, dip pickerel in the batter, then, using tongs, carefully lower it into the hot oil. Repeat until the pan is full but not overcrowded. (Work in batches if necessary, bringing the oil back up to temperature in between.) Fry pickerel until the batter is golden brown, about 5 minutes. Using tongs or a slotted spoon, transfer the fish to the paper bag–lined plate to drain.

TO SERVE Divide hot pickerel tempura evenly among eight warmed plates. Serve immediately with a bowl of wasabi-ginger tartar sauce on the side.

Serves 8

WASABI-GINGER TARTAR SAUCE

1½ cups mayonnaise

Juice of ½ lemon

¼ cup finely chopped gherkins

¼ cup finely chopped capers

¼ cup pickled ginger, chopped

1 Tbsp wasabi powder

1 Tbsp pickled ginger juice (reserved from the jar of pickled ginger)

PICKEREL TEMPURA

3 egg yolks

1 cup ice water

1 cup all-purpose flour

¾ cup cornstarch

6 to 8 cups vegetable oil

2 lbs skinless pickerel fillets, deboned and cut in 2-inch chunks

Smoked Sablefish Cakes with Fruit Chutney and Spicy Greens

SCOTT POHORELIC, River Café, Calgary

SABLEFISH Alaska, British Columbia: *Best choice*; California, Oregon, Washington: *Some concerns*

1 Tbsp olive oil

1 Tbsp minced shallots

1 tsp minced garlic

2 Tbsp slivered red onions

2 lbs cold-smoked sablefish, finely diced

1 cup cooked wild rice

1 Tbsp minced red bell pepper

2 Tbsp chopped fresh herbs, such as oregano and Italian flat-leaf parsley

2 tsp sesame seeds, toasted

¼ cup mayonnaise

1½ cups bread crumbs

1 tsp sesame oil

1 cup all-purpose flour

2 eggs, beaten

¼ cup canola oil

½ cup peach or mango chutney, for garnish

4 cups arugula or watercress, washed and shredded, for garnish

Heat olive oil in a frying pan on medium-low heat. Add shallots, garlic, and red onions and sauté slowly until tender, about 8 minutes. Remove from the heat and allow to cool.

In a medium bowl, thoroughly combine the onion mixture, sablefish, wild rice, red peppers, herbs, sesame seeds, mayonnaise, ½ cup of the bread crumbs, and sesame oil. Season with salt and pepper. Using a spoon or your hands, form 16 patties, each 2½ inches in diameter and ¾ inch thick. Arrange patties on a small baking sheet and place them in the freezer for about 15 minutes, or until they begin to firm up.

Place flour, eggs, and the remaining bread crumbs in three separate shallow dishes. Remove chilled patties from the freezer and dredge in flour. Dip patties in the egg, then coat them with bread crumbs.

Line a plate with a paper bag. Heat canola oil in a frying pan on medium heat. Add sablefish cakes and pan-fry on one side until golden brown, 5 to 7 minutes. Turn cakes over and cook until browned, about 10 more minutes. Transfer to the paper bag–lined plate and allow to drain.

TO SERVE Arrange two sablefish cakes on each individual plate. Serve with a dollop of peach (or mango) chutney and a handful of arugula (or watercress).

Serves 8 as a first course

Tojo's Marinated Sablefish

HIDEKAZU TOJO, Tojo's Restaurant, Vancouver

SABLEFISH Alaska, British Columbia: *Best choice*; California, Oregon, Washington: *Some concerns*

In a small bowl, combine soy sauce, mirin (or sake or white wine), sugar, and ginger until well mixed. Pour the marinade into a large, clean food-grade plastic bag (or a plastic container, with a lid, that is just large enough to hold the fish). Add sablefish fillets, pushing them into the marinade. Squeeze out as much air as possible and seal the bag tightly with an elastic band, close to the fish (or put the lid on the plastic container). Refrigerate overnight or for up to 2 days.

Preheat the oven to 450°F. Lightly grease a baking sheet. Pat dry the sablefish fillets, then place them on the baking sheet. Discard the marinade. Bake the fillets until the fish is cooked through and flakes easily, 10 to 12 minutes.

While the fish is cooking, heat the olive oil in a frying pan on high heat. Add spinach and garlic and stir until the greens are wilted. Remove from the heat and season with salt and pepper.

TO SERVE Divide the spinach among four warmed plates. Top with a sablefish fillet and serve immediately.

Serves 4 as a first course

1/3 cup dark soy sauce

1/4 cup mirin or sake or white wine

1 Tbsp granulated sugar

2 tsp ground ginger

4 skinless sablefish fillets (each 3 oz)

2 tsp olive oil

1 bunch spinach, washed and tough stems removed, if necessary

1 tsp grated garlic

Portuguese Seafood Stew with Sablefish (*Caldeirada da marisco*)

DAVID BESTON, Jericho Tennis Club, Vancouver

SABLEFISH Alaska, British Columbia: *Best choice;*
California, Oregon, Washington: *Some concerns*

MUSSELS Farmed: *Best choice;* Wild: *Some concerns*

SQUID *Best choice*

SPOT PRAWNS *Best choice*

6 Tbsp extra-virgin olive oil

4 cloves garlic, chopped

1 Tbsp cumin seeds, roasted and ground

1 small onion, diced

1½ cups dry white wine, such as Vinho Verde

4 cups chicken stock

6 small Yukon Gold potatoes, in 1-inch dice

1 chorizo sausage (4 oz), cooked, cut in half lengthwise, then in ¼-inch slices

2 ripe tomatoes, coarsely chopped

In a large wide saucepan or a stockpot, heat 3 Tbsp of the olive oil on medium-high heat. Add garlic and cumin and sauté until fragrant, 1 to 2 minutes. Reduce the heat to medium-low, add onions and cook until translucent, 3 to 4 minutes.

Deglaze the pan with white wine. Increase the heat to high. Boil to reduce by three quarters, about 2 minutes, then stir in chicken stock. Reduce the heat to medium and bring to a simmer. Add potatoes, chorizo, and tomatoes and simmer until potatoes are cooked through, 12 to 15 minutes.

Add mussels, squid, and prawns, cover and simmer gently until mussels open, 2 to 5 minutes. Stir in paprika and parsley, then remove from the heat.

Season sablefish with sea salt and ground black pepper. In a separate frying pan, heat the remaining olive oil on medium-high heat. Place fillets, skin side down, in the pan and sear until skin is golden and crispy, about 3 minutes. Reduce the heat to medium and turn the fillets over. Cook for 4 minutes, or until the fish is firm and opaque. Transfer the sablefish to a plate. Cover and keep warm.

Return the pan to the heat and add kale. Season with sea salt and ground black pepper and cook, stirring often, until the greens are wilted, about 3 minutes. (If the kale sticks to the pan, deglaze the pan with 2 Tbsp of the broth.)

TO SERVE Spoon the broth into six warmed bowls, evenly dividing the seafood, sausage, and potatoes among them. Place a mound of wilted kale in the centre of each bowl and top with a sablefish fillet, skin side up. Drizzle each serving with ½ teaspoon of olive oil and serve with generous helpings of crusty bread.

Serves 6

24 mussels, cleaned and beards snipped off

½ lb cleaned squid (including tentacles), sliced into rings

½ lb prawn tails

1 Tbsp smoked paprika (sweet)

1 Tbsp chopped fresh Italian flat-leaf parsley

6 sablefish fillets (each 4 oz), skin on, scaled

½ lb kale, separated into leaves, tough stems removed

3 tsp high-quality extra-virgin olive oil, to finish

Baked Sablefish with Roasted Beets, Buttered Chard, and Goat Cheese Cream

ROBERT CLARK, C Restaurant, Nu Restaurant, and Raincity Grill, Vancouver

SABLEFISH Alaska, British Columbia: *Best choice*;
California, Oregon, Washington: *Some concerns*

BAKED SABLEFISH
6 sablefish fillets
(each 5 oz), skin on

1 cup cold water

1 tsp granulated sugar

1 tsp sea salt

2 Tbsp honey

2 Tbsp pepitas (shelled
pumpkin seeds), toasted

BAKED SABLEFISH Arrange sablefish in a single layer in a shallow dish just large enough to hold all of the fillets. Place water in a small bowl, then add sugar and sea salt. Stir until dissolved. Pour this liquid over the sablefish, making sure to cover the fillets completely. Cover the dish with parchment paper and refrigerate for 1 hour. Remove fish and pat dry. Discard liquid.

Coat a large plate with honey. Place fish, flesh side down, in honey. Allow to stand at room temperature for 30 minutes.

Preheat the oven to 400°F. Line a baking sheet with parchment paper. Using a slotted spoon, remove sablefish from the honey and transfer, skin side down, to the baking sheet. Sprinkle with pumpkin seeds. Bake until the tip of a knife inserted in the thickest part of the fish comes out warm, 7 to 10 minutes.

VEGETABLES Heat walnut oil in a frying pan on medium heat. Add beets and stir until hot, then add red wine vinegar and walnuts and remove from the heat. Cover to keep warm.

In another frying pan, melt butter on medium-high heat. Add chard and season with salt and ground pepper. Stir often until wilted, 7 to 10 minutes.

GOAT CHEESE CREAM In a saucepan, bring cream to a boil on medium heat. Whisk in goat cheese and lemon juice until the sauce coats the back of a spoon. If the sauce is too thick, stir in a little water.

TO SERVE Arrange beets and chard on six warmed plates. Top each serving with a sablefish fillet, then drizzle with goat cheese cream.

Serves 6

VEGETABLES
2 Tbsp walnut oil

2 cups diced,
cooked baby beets

1 Tbsp red wine vinegar

½ cup walnuts, toasted

2 Tbsp butter

2 bunches Swiss chard,
trimmed and thickly sliced

GOAT CHEESE CREAM
½ cup whipping cream

½ cup crumbled
fresh goat cheese

1 Tbsp fresh lemon juice

Braised Sablefish in a Chanterelle Butter Sauce

RUSTY PENNO, Boffins Club, Saskatoon

SABLEFISH Alaska, British Columbia: *Best choice*;
California, Oregon, Washington: *Some concerns*

4 Tbsp canola oil

4 sablefish fillets
(each 5 oz), skin on

4 oz fresh-picked
chanterelle mushrooms,
in quarters

12 cippolini
onions, roasted

12 new Russian Blue
potatoes, parboiled

1 cup light chicken stock
or vegetable stock

2 to 4 oz cold
butter, in cubes

Preheat the oven to 375°F.

Heat canola oil in a large ovenproof frying pan on medium-high heat. Place sablefish, skin side down, in the pan and sear for 1 to 2 minutes, or until skin is crispy. Transfer the fillets to a plate and set aside.

Add mushrooms, onions, and potatoes to the frying pan and sauté until tender, 8 to 10 minutes. Add chicken (or vegetable) stock and heat until it simmers, about 10 minutes. Add sablefish, skin side up, then transfer to the oven and bake for 8 to 10 minutes. Remove from the oven and transfer fillets to a separate plate. Use a slotted spoon to divide the potatoes, onions, and mushrooms evenly among four individual bowls or plates. Top each serving with a sablefish fillet.

Return the pan to high heat and reduce the braising liquid by half, about 5 minutes. Remove from the heat, whisk in butter until well incorporated, then season with salt and pepper.

TO SERVE Spoon the sauce on and around the sablefish. Serve immediately.

Serves 4

Salmon and Edamame Salad with Wasabi Mayonnaise

KAREN BARNABY, The Fish House in Stanley Park, Vancouver

SALMON Pacific, wild: *Some concerns*; Farmed: *Avoid*

In a bowl, mix together salmon, edamame, celery, and green onions.

In another bowl, combine mayonnaise and wasabi paste to taste. Gently fold into the salmon mixture. Turn into a serving bowl, then cover and refrigerate to allow the flavours to meld, about 30 minutes.

TO SERVE Divide the salad among four plates, then garnish with sesame seeds and ginger.

Serves 4

1 can (7 oz) pink salmon, well drained (and bones discarded, if you prefer)

1 cup shelled edamame (fresh soy beans), cooked and chilled

½ cup finely diced celery

2 green onions, white and green parts, thinly sliced

⅓ cup mayonnaise

2 tsp wasabi paste

1 Tbsp sesame seeds, toasted, for garnish

1 Tbsp julienned fresh ginger, for garnish

Salmon and Shrimp Cakes
with Blueberry Pear Salsa

JOHN BISHOP, Bishop's, Vancouver

SALMON Pacific, wild: *Some concerns*; Farmed: *Avoid*

SHRIMP Trap-caught: *Best choice*;
Trawled: *Some concerns*; Warm-water: *Avoid*

BLUEBERRY PEAR SALSA
2 Tbsp chopped fresh
cilantro leaves

3 Tbsp finely diced red onion

1 ripe pear, peeled, cored,
and diced (about ½ cup)

1 cup fresh blueberries

2 Tbsp fresh lime juice

Pinch of salt

SALMON AND
SHRIMP CAKES
¾ lb skinless salmon
fillet, deboned

5 Tbsp vegetable oil

1 cup fresh bread crumbs

½ lb baby
shrimp, peeled

2 Tbsp chopped fresh
Italian flat-leaf parsley

½ cup light mayonnaise

½ tsp freshly
ground pepper

1 green onion, white and
green parts, chopped

1 tsp finely grated
lemon zest

½ cup cornmeal

½ cup all-purpose flour

BLUEBERRY PEAR SALSA In a bowl, combine all ingredients until well mixed. Refrigerate for 2 hours to allow the flavours to blend.

SALMON AND SHRIMP CAKES Season salmon fillet with salt and pepper and rub with 1 Tbsp of the vegetable oil. In a frying pan on medium-high heat or on a barbecue set to medium, sear salmon for 10 minutes per side. Set aside to cool.

Using a fork, flake salmon into small chunks and place in a large bowl. Add bread crumbs, shrimp, parsley, mayonnaise, pepper, green onions, 2 Tbsp of the vegetable oil, and lemon zest. Combine well. Using a spoon or your hands, form 4 individual patties.

Combine cornmeal and flour in a small shallow bowl. Dip patties in the cornmeal mixture, patting the coating onto the cakes until well covered.

Preheat a cast-iron frying pan on medium heat. Add the remaining vegetable oil and cakes and gently cook for 10 minutes per side, or until completely warmed through and lightly browned.

TO SERVE Place one salmon and shrimp cake on each plate. Top with salsa and serve immediately.

Serves 4

Fast Fish Hash

DOLLY WATTS, cookbook author, Port Alberni, British Columbia

SALMON Pacific, wild: *Some concerns*; Farmed: *Avoid*

Heat canola oil in a frying pan on medium heat. Add onions and potatoes and sauté until lightly browned, about 5 minutes. Add salmon and cook until fish is heated through, about 5 minutes. Sprinkle with celery salt, white pepper, and basil.

TO SERVE Divide fish hash between two warmed plates and enjoy.

Serves 2

2 Tbsp canola oil

½ cup diced onions

2 cups peeled, diced potatoes

½ lb salmon, cooked, in bite-size pieces

¼ tsp celery salt

¼ tsp white pepper

Pinch of dried basil

Celebration Salmon

JENNIFER DANTER, *Chatelaine* magazine

SALMON Pacific, wild: *Some concerns*; Farmed: *Avoid*

GARLIC-BASIL OIL

1 cup olive oil

4 cloves garlic, thinly sliced

¼ tsp salt

⅓ cup shredded fresh basil

¼ cup pine nuts or slivered almonds, toasted, for garnish

BARBECUED SALMON

1 whole salmon (6 to 8 lbs), cleaned and skin on, scaled (head and tail removed, if you prefer)

4 green onions, white and green parts, coarsely chopped

1 lemon, thinly sliced

1 piece fresh ginger (about 1 inch), peeled and thinly sliced

2 Tbsp olive oil

2 lemons, in 6 wedges

GARLIC-BASIL OIL Heat olive oil in a small saucepan on medium heat. When oil is warm but not hot, remove from the heat and stir in garlic, salt and pinches of ground black pepper. Gently fold in basil. Set aside until ready to use. (Note that garlic preserved in oil can be a health risk if stored improperly; discard any garlic-basil oil not used in this recipe.)

BARBECUED SALMON Generously oil the barbecue grill. Preheat the barbecue to medium.

Under cold running water, rinse salmon, inside and out, then pat dry with a clean tea towel. Stuff the cavity with green onions, lemon, and ginger and sprinkle with salt and pepper. To prevent the stuffing from falling out, tie the salmon closed with butcher twine or insert a few metal skewers to close the cavity. Brush the outside of the salmon with olive oil.

Position salmon on the front part of the grill with the backbone facing away from you (this will make turning the salmon easier). Grill on one side until the skin is crisp and the fish is cooked through to the bone, 6 to 15 minutes, depending on the thickness of the salmon. (Insert a knife into the thickest part of the fish. If the tip comes out

warm, the salmon is done. Or, insert an instant-
read thermometer into thickest part of the fish.
It should read 120°F to 125°F. A good rule of
thumb is to cook whole salmon about 10 minutes
per inch.)

Using two large wide spatulas, turn the
salmon away from you in one motion. Don't
worry if some of the skin sticks or peels off.
Grill for another 6 to 15 minutes, or until cooked
through. Carefully transfer the salmon to a
large platter. Remove the twine or skewers. Discard the green onions, lemon slices, and ginger.

With your fingers, grasp the backbone at the
head end of the fish and gently but firmly lift it
out, pulling the long bones along with it. Discard
the bones. The salmon will open into two long
halves. Remove any remaining bones with
tweezers and discard.

TO SERVE Arrange the salmon, skin side down,
on a serving platter. Drizzle with the garlic-basil
oil and sprinkle with pine nuts or almonds.
Serve immediately with a bowl of lemon wedges.

Serves 10 to 12

Cedar-planked Salmon with Soy-Ginger Glaze

JANE RODMELL, *Cottage Life* magazine

SALMON Pacific, wild: *Some concerns*; Farmed: *Avoid*

SOY-GINGER GLAZE

½ cup soy sauce

¼ cup dry sherry

¼ cup peanut oil
or vegetable oil

¼ cup brown sugar,
lightly packed

2 cloves garlic,
finely chopped

2 green onions,
white and green parts,
finely chopped

2 tsp freshly grated ginger

CEDAR-PLANKED SALMON

1 untreated cedar plank,
roughly 8 × 16 inches
and ¾ to 1 inch thick,
soaked in water for 1 hour
(or preferably overnight)

1 Tbsp vegetable oil

2 salmon fillets
(each about 1½ lbs),
skin on

1 Tbsp finely chopped
fresh cilantro or Italian
flat-leaf parsley, for garnish

NOTE To submerge the plank in water, weigh it down with a brick or heavy cans. You can use the same plank several times; just scrub it after cooking and soak it before each use. Discard it when it becomes too charred. A scrap of cedar from the woodpile or the lumberyard works well, but cedar planks especially for grilling are sold in some supermarkets and kitchenware stores.

SOY-GINGER GLAZE In a small saucepan on medium heat, combine glaze ingredients. Simmer for 5 minutes, stirring until sugar dissolves. Remove from the heat and allow to cool.

Strain the glaze through a fine-mesh sieve, discarding any solids. Will keep refrigerated in an airtight container for up to 1 month. This glaze can also be used to baste ribs, wings, chicken, pork, shrimp, and tuna.

CEDAR-PLANKED SALMON Pat dry the cedar plank and brush one side of it very lightly with vegetable oil.

Place salmon on a plate, skin side down, and brush with half of the soy-ginger glaze. Set aside for 15 minutes.

Preheat a grill or a barbecue to high. Fill a spray bottle with water.

Place the plank on the grill, oiled side up. Close the lid, reduce the heat to medium, and heat for about 10 minutes, until the plank begins to smell smoky and the wood starts to snap and crackle.

Lift the lid and carefully slide the salmon fillets, skin side down, onto the plank. Close the lid and grill the salmon for 5 to 7 minutes. (Check regularly to be sure the plank has not caught fire; spray any flames with water.) Brush with most of the remaining glaze, then cook for 5 to 7 minutes more, or until the fish flakes when tested. (You do not need to turn the fillets.)

TO SERVE For a rustic presentation, carefully lift the plank from the grill, brush the salmon with a little extra glaze, sprinkle it with the cilantro (or parsley), and serve at the table on the plank. Or, use a large, flat lifter to separate the fish from the skin and gently slide the whole fillets onto a serving platter.

Serves 6

Lemon-cured Sardines on Angel Hair Pasta with Tomato Fennel Ragout

ANDREA LEUNG, The Fairmont Waterfront Hotel, Vancouver

Third-place winner, SeaChoice Culinary Competition

SARDINES *Best choice*

TOMATO FENNEL RAGOUT

¼ cup olive oil

½ cup chopped onions

2 pints cherry tomatoes, cut in half

1 cup diced ripe tomatoes

1 cup diced fennel

1 sprig thyme, whole

1 bay leaf

1 clove garlic, chopped

1 Tbsp white wine vinegar

CURED SARDINES

1 cup kosher salt

1 cup granulated sugar

2 Tbsp lemon zest

3 sprigs Italian flat-leaf parsley, whole

12 sardine fillets (each 2 to 3 oz), skin on

2 Tbsp olive oil

TOMATO FENNEL RAGOUT Heat olive oil in a heavy-bottomed saucepan on medium-high heat. Add onions, cherry and diced tomatoes, fennel, thyme, bay leaf, and garlic. Sauté, stirring often, until the vegetables are soft, 5 to 10 minutes. Add white wine vinegar, reduce the heat to low, and continue to cook for 1 hour, stirring occasionally. If the mixture seems too thick, add water, a tablespoon at a time, until the desired consistency is reached. Season to taste with salt and pepper.

CURED SARDINES In a small bowl, mix kosher salt, sugar, lemon zest, and parsley. Sprinkle half the salt mixture on a large plate; lay the sardine fillets on top. Cover the fillets with the remaining salt mixture and allow to cure for 30 minutes.

Remove the fillets from the salt mixture and rinse thoroughly under cold running water. Pat dry.

Heat olive oil in a large frying pan on medium-high heat. Add sardines, skin side down, and sauté until golden brown, about 2 minutes. Turn the fillets over and finish cooking for about 1 minute. Remove from the heat.

PASTA Bring a large pot of salted water to a boil on medium-high heat. Cook pasta according to the package directions, then drain pasta and return it to the pot. Add the tomato fennel ragout and toss until well coated.

TO SERVE Divide the pasta among six plates. Top each serving with two sardine fillets, then sprinkle with feta and pine nuts.

Serves 6

PASTA

1 lb angel hair pasta

¼ cup feta cheese, for garnish

2 Tbsp pine nuts, toasted, for garnish

Crispy Lemon Sardines
with Parmesan and Oregano

KAREN BARNABY, The Fish House in Stanley Park, Vancouver

SARDINES *Best choice*

3/4 cup panko
(Japanese bread crumbs)

1/4 tsp sea salt

1/4 tsp freshly
ground black pepper

1/2 cup grated Parmesan
cheese

1/2 tsp dried oregano

1/2 cup mayonnaise

1 clove garlic, minced

1 tsp grated lemon zest

1 Tbsp fresh lemon juice

12 sardine fillets
(each 3 to 4 oz), skin on

Preheat the oven to 425°F. Line a deep baking sheet with parchment paper.

In a large shallow dish, combine panko, sea salt, pepper, Parmesan cheese, and oregano. In a shallow bowl, stir together mayonnaise, garlic, lemon zest, and lemon juice.

Dip the flesh side of each sardine into the mayonnaise mixture, then press it into the panko mixture. Arrange sardines, coated side up, on the baking sheet. Bake until crispy and golden, 10 to 15 minutes.

TO SERVE Arrange three fillets on each warmed plate. Serve immediately.

Serves 4

Applewood-smoked Sturgeon with
Gala Apple Confit and Parsnip Purée

MICHAEL HOWELL, Tempest Restaurant, Wolfville, Nova Scotia

STURGEON North American, farmed: *Best choice*;
North American, wild: *Some concerns*; Russian, Iranian, wild: *Avoid*

SMOKED STURGEON Place applewood chips in a wood smoker or a barbecue. Preheat to medium-high.

Place sturgeon fillets in the smoker (or on the grill). Smoke sturgeon until almost cooked through, but not quite, about 1 hour. (If using a barbecue, prepare the parsnip purée first. Grill fillets on one side for 6 minutes, then turn over and grill the other side for another 6 minutes.) When done, the outside of the fillets should be golden.

Transfer the fillets to a large cutting board. Using a sharp knife, slice the fish as thinly as possible. Cover and set aside.

PARSNIP PURÉE Place parsnips and a pinch of salt in a saucepan, cover with water and bring to a boil on medium-high heat. Cook until quite soft, about 15 minutes. Drain, reserving 1 cup of the cooking liquid.

Return the saucepan of parsnips to the heat. Add cream and heat until warm. Allow to cool slightly, then pour parsnips and cream into a blender or food processor. Add butter and purée until the mixture is completely smooth. (If the mixture is too thick, add some of the cooking liquid.) Season with salt and Tabasco. Return the purée to the saucepan. Cover and keep warm.

Continued overleaf…

SMOKED STURGEON
applewood chips

6 skinless farmed sturgeon fillets (each 5 to 6 oz)

3 cups frisée or microgreens, for garnish

PARSNIP PURÉE
3 parsnips, peeled and chopped

¼ cup whipping cream

1 Tbsp butter

Dashes of Tabasco sauce

APPLE CONFIT

1 Tbsp duck fat or
bacon fat or butter

2 Gala apples,
peeled, cored,
and diced

1 tsp finely
chopped chives

APPLE CONFIT Line a plate with a paper bag.
Melt duck fat (or bacon fat or butter) in a cast-iron
pan on medium-high heat. Add apples and sauté,
stirring constantly, until golden, 2 to 3 minutes.
Transfer to the paper bag–lined plate to drain.

In a small bowl, toss apples with chives.
Set aside.

TO SERVE Place a small mound of parsnip purée
onto the middle of six plates. Spoon some warm
apple confit over it. Fan several slices of the sturgeon over the apple confit. Garnish each plate
with a small handful of frisée (or microgreens).

Serves 6

Grilled Swordfish with Forbidden Black Rice and Soy Emulsion

TED GRANT, Gio, Halifax

SWORDFISH Atlantic Canada, harpoon: *Best choice*;
US Atlantic, pelagic long-line: *Some concerns*;
Canada, Mediterranean, Southeast Atlantic pelagic long-line: *Avoid*

SOY EMULSION In a small frying pan, heat vegetable oil on medium heat. Add shallot and garlic and cook until golden, about 4 minutes. Add soy sauce, rice vinegar, honey, and peppercorns, then boil until reduced by half, about 5 minutes. Add chicken stock, boil and reduce by half again, about 5 minutes. Strain through a fine-mesh sieve and discard any solids. Return emulsion to the frying pan and reserve in a warm place.

GRILLED SWORDFISH Arrange fish fillets in a single layer in a baking dish. Cover with ginger, lime juice, tamari, and cilantro. Turn fish until evenly coated. Cover and refrigerate for 1 hour.

continued overleaf…

SOY EMULSION
1 tsp vegetable oil

1 shallot, coarsely chopped

1 clove garlic, minced

1/4 cup light soy sauce

1/8 cup rice vinegar

1 tsp honey

1 tsp black peppercorns

1 cup roasted chicken stock, reduced to 1/2 cup

1/2 lb cold unsalted butter, in cubes

GRILLED SWORDFISH
4 skinless swordfish fillets (each 6 oz)

1/2 cup sliced ginger

Juice of 1 lime

1/4 cup tamari

2 Tbps chopped cilantro

FORBIDDEN RICE

1 cup forbidden black rice
or long-grain white rice

1 Tbsp vegetable oil

2 Tbsp finely
chopped ginger

2 cloves garlic, minced

1 small shallot, minced

8 baby bok choy,
cut in halves

½ lb oyster mushrooms

1 cup snow peas,
trimmed

½ cup cooked and
shucked edamame
(fresh soy beans)

½ cup fish sauce

FORBIDDEN RICE Place rice in a large saucepan with 2½ cups water. Bring to a boil on high heat, then reduce the heat to low, cover and simmer until tender, about 40 minutes. Allow to stand, covered, 10 minutes, then fluff with a fork.

Heat vegetable oil in a very large wide frying pan on medium-high heat. Add ginger, garlic, and shallot. Stir for 1 minute, then add bok choy, mushrooms, snow peas, and edamame. Stir-fry until tender-crisp, about 4 minutes, then add fish sauce. Stir to mix evenly, then pour vegetables over rice and stir gently to combine.

FINISH FISH Preheat the barbecue to medium-high.

Place fish fillets on the grill and cook for 4 to 6 minutes per side, until fish is just cooked through. Discard the marinade.

FINISH EMULSION Bring emulsion back to a boil on medium heat, then remove from the heat and whisk in butter until evenly mixed.

TO SERVE Mound warm rice in the centre of four plates. Top each serving with a fillet of fish and drizzle with soy emulsion.

Serves 4

Tilapia Piccata with Asparagus

BONNIE STERN, The Bonnie Stern School of Cooking, Toronto

TILAPIA North American, farmed: *Best choice;*
Chinese, Taiwanese, farmed: *Avoid*

Season tilapia on both sides with salt and freshly
ground black pepper and lightly dust with flour.
Heat olive oil in a large frying pan on medium-
high heat. Arrange fish in a single layer and
pan-fry for 3 minutes. (If the frying pan is not big
enough to hold all of the tilapia, cook the fillets in
batches, adding more oil as necessary to stop the
fish from sticking.) Turn fillets over and cook
for 3 minutes more, or until fish just flakes at the
thickest part when lightly separated with the back
of a spoon. Transfer to a serving dish and cover
with a lid to keep warm.

Wipe out the pan, then return it to the heat.
Add 1 Tbsp of the butter. When butter is melted
and foamy, add asparagus and sprinkle with
pinches of salt and pepper. Stir-fry until bright
green, 3 to 5 minutes. Add a few spoonfuls of
water if necessary to stop any burning. Spoon
asparagus over fish.

Return the pan to the heat once more and
add lemon juice and white wine (or chicken stock
or water). Boil, stirring constantly, until reduced
by half, 1 to 2 minutes. Stir in the remaining butter.

TO SERVE Spoon the sauce over the tilapia and
asparagus, and garnish with lemon slices.

Serves 4

4 skinless tilapia fillets
(about 1 lb in total)

2 Tbsp all-purpose flour

2 Tbsp olive oil

2 Tbsp butter, cold

½ lb asparagus, trimmed
and cut in 2-inch pieces

3 Tbsp fresh lemon juice

3 Tbsp dry white wine or
chicken stock or water

4 slices lemon, for garnish

Tomato-Anchovy Tilapia "en Papillote"

STEVE WALL, The Whalesbone Oyster House, Ottawa

TILAPIA North American, farmed: *Best choice*;
Chinese, Taiwanese, farmed: *Avoid*

1 can (19 oz) whole tomatoes with juice

2 Tbsp balsamic vinegar

1 tsp granulated sugar

6 to 8 canned anchovy fillets, rinsed

¼ lb unsalted butter, at room temperature and cut in small cubes

1 small bulb fennel, thinly shaved or sliced

1 leek, white part only, sliced in ¼-inch rings and washed

½ head garlic, roasted and peel discarded

4 skinless tilapia fillets (each 6 oz)

¼ cup dry white wine

Pour the tomato juice into a small saucepan. Using a sharp knife, slice open tomatoes and drain their juice into the pan as well. Reserve the tomatoes in a small bowl. Add balsamic vinegar and sugar to the tomato juice. Bring to a simmer on medium heat and cook, stirring often, until liquid has reduced by three quarters, about 5 minutes.

Finely chop tomatoes and anchovies, then place in a medium bowl. Pour in the warm tomato reduction. Add butter and stir until evenly mixed. Set aside.

Preheat the oven to 400°F. Cut 4 sheets of parchment paper, each 12 × 14 inches. Fold each sheet of parchment paper in half to make a rectangle of 12 × 7 inches. Arrange the paper rectangles, short side toward you and folded edges on the left, on a work surface. With a pencil and starting at the top left-hand corner of each rectangle, draw a half-heart shape, using as much of the rectangle as possible. Use scissors to cut out the shapes. Open the folded paper and set the heart shapes on a clean work surface. Make sure there's enough room to hold the fillets once the paper is folded over them.

On the bottom half of each paper heart, arrange ¼ of the fennel, leek, and garlic. Top with a tilapia fillet and sprinkle with salt and pepper. Spoon a generous dollop of the tomato-anchovy butter over the fish.

Fold the top half of the parchment paper over the filling. To seal the open sides, begin at one corner and, holding the top and bottom sheets together, pinch the sheets between your fingers, overlapping them to create 5 or 6 folds, or pleats, along each edge. Before sealing completely, pour 1 Tbsp of the white wine into each package. Seal the 4 packages and arrange on a baking sheet. Bake in the centre of the oven until the tilapia is cooked through and the paper starts to brown, about 15 minutes.

TO SERVE Place a parchment-paper package on each warmed plate. Carefully open the pouches (the steam is very hot), enjoy the wonderful aroma, and savour the tilapia and the vegetables.

Serves 4

Smoked Rainbow Trout Gougères

SCOTT POHORELIC, River Café, Calgary

RAINBOW TROUT Farmed: *Best choice;*
Wild: *See Freshwater Fish, page 167*

HERBED CRÈME FRAÎCHE
2 cups crème fraîche
or sour cream

2 Tbsp chopped fresh
Italian flat-leaf parsley

2 Tbsp chopped fresh mint

2 Tbsp chopped fresh
tarragon

2 Tbsp chopped chives

Zest of 2 lemons

1 Tbsp grainy mustard

1 Tbsp maple syrup

NOTE Cunningham's cold-smoked rainbow trout is perfect for this dish.

HERBED CRÈME FRAÎCHE In a medium bowl, combine crème fraîche (or sour cream), parsley, mint, tarragon, chives, lemon zest, grainy mustard, and maple syrup. Season with salt and pepper. Will keep refrigerated in an airtight container for up to 5 days.

GOUGÈRES Preheat the oven to 425°F. Line a baking sheet with parchment paper.

In a saucepan on medium-high heat, combine milk, water, and butter. Bring to a simmer, then add flour, salt, and sugar. Reduce the heat to low and mix thoroughly with a wooden spoon. Continue to cook until the mixture thickens and begins to pull away from the sides of the saucepan, about 3 minutes. Remove the mixture from the heat and allow it to cool slightly.

Transfer the dough to the bowl of an electric mixer fitted with a paddle attachment. With the motor running at slow speed, add 1 egg and mix until well combined. Add the remaining eggs, one at a time, until well incorporated. (If you don't have an electric mixer, you can beat in the eggs by hand but this requires a little stamina.) Add Gouda cheese and mix just enough to combine.

Drop teaspoonfuls of the dough onto the baking sheet. You should have 30 to 40. Bake for 10 minutes, then reduce the heat to 325°F. Open the oven door for 1 minute, then close it and continue to bake for another 10 minutes, or until the gougères are puffed up and golden brown. Remove from the oven and allow to cool. (Do not refrigerate the gougères or they will become soggy.)

TO SERVE Slice each gougère in half horizontally, cutting most of the way through but leaving one edge intact. Open the gougères and top each one with a dollop of the crème fraîche, a few greens, and a slice of smoked trout.

Serves 10 as a first course

GOUGÈRES

½ cup milk

1/2 cup water

6 Tbsp butter

1 cup white bread flour

¼ tsp salt

1 tsp granulated sugar

4 eggs

¾ cup grated Gouda cheese

1½ lbs smoked trout, very thinly sliced

1 bunch peppery greens, such as watercress or arugula, washed, dried, and torn in small pieces

Dandelion Tea-cured Steelhead Trout

RUSTY PENNO, Boffins Club, Saskatoon

STEELHEAD TROUT Inland farmed: *Best choice;*
Wild: *See Freshwater Fish, page* 167

1 cup kosher or sea salt

2 Tbsp granulated sugar

¼ cup whole
green tea leaves

¼ cup dried dandelion
leaves (available at
health food stores)

Zest of 2 lemons, chopped

1 Tbsp crushed black
peppercorns

2 lbs center-cut steelhead
or rainbow trout fillets, skin
on and pin bones removed

30 crackers or slices of
toasted French baguette

⅓ cup crème fraîche,
for garnish

2 Tbsp chopped fresh
herbs, such as dill or
fennel, for garnish

Cut 2 pieces of plastic wrap or butcher paper,
each 12 × 24 inches.

In a small bowl, combine kosher (or sea) salt,
sugar, green tea, dandelion leaves, lemon zest,
and peppercorns. Rub both sides of the trout fillets heavily with about half of the spice mixture.

Lay 1 sheet of the plastic wrap (or butcher
paper), short side toward you, on a clean work
surface and sprinkle with half of the remaining
spice mixture. Arrange all of the trout, skin side
down, in the middle of the plastic wrap
(or butcher paper), then sprinkle with the remaining spice mixture. Fold the top half of the plastic
wrap (or butcher paper) over the fillets, then
the bottom half over the top. Fold in the sides
like an envelope.

Lay the second sheet, short side toward you,
on the work surface. Place the wrapped package
in the middle of it. Repeat the folding so the package is completely sealed and no juices will escape.

Place the wrapped package in a large resealable plastic bag, remove as much air as possible,
then seal the bag. Set the resealable plastic bag in a
shallow baking dish, cover it with a small cutting

board or a piece of cardboard cut to fit, then
weight it with 5 to 7 lbs. Two very large cans
(or 5 to 6 smaller ones) work well. Refrigerate for
12 hours, turning the bag once after 6 hours.

Remove the package from the bag, unwrap
it, and rinse trout under cold water. Dry with a
clean tea towel. Place fillets on a cutting board and
use a sharp knife to slice very thinly at a 45-degree
angle, stopping at the skin. Slice only what you
plan to serve.

TO SERVE Arrange crackers (or toasted baguette
slices) on a serving platter. Top each one with a
slice of trout. Garnish with a ½ tsp of the crème
fraîche and sprinkle with chopped fresh herbs.

NOTE The trout will keep refrigerated and
wrapped tightly in the resealable plastic bag
for about a week, or frozen for 1 month.

Serves 10 to 15 as a first course

Crispy Fried Trout Fillets
with Red Pepper Mayonnaise

CINDA CHAVICH, cookbook author, Calgary

RAINBOW TROUT Farmed: *Best choice;*
Wild: *See Freshwater Fish, page 167*

RED PEPPER MAYONNAISE
½ cup mayonnaise

2 Tbsp plain yogurt
or sour cream

1 red bell pepper, roasted,
peeled, and seeded

1 Tbsp fresh lime juice

¼ tsp ground cumin

1 green onion, green and
white parts, chopped

½ tsp hot chili sauce

CRISPY TROUT
¼ cup milk

¼ cup plain yogurt

1 egg, beaten

1 tsp Dijon mustard

½ tsp paprika

½ cup all-purpose flour

¼ cup cornmeal

¼ tsp cayenne pepper

4 skinless trout fillets
(each 8 oz), deboned

¼ cup canola oil, or more

1 lemon, in 4 wedges

RED PEPPER MAYONNAISE Combine all ingredients in a food processor and purée until smooth. Transfer to a bowl and refrigerate until needed. Will keep refrigerated in an airtight container for 3 days.

CRISPY TROUT In a medium bowl, whisk together milk, yogurt, egg, Dijon mustard, and paprika. Season with salt and pepper. In a shallow dish, combine flour, cornmeal, and cayenne. Dip trout into the milk mixture, then roll in the cornmeal coating. Arrange coated trout fillets in a single layer on a baking sheet and refrigerate for 10 minutes.

Heat canola oil in a large frying pan on medium-high heat until hot but not smoking. Pan-fry trout for 2 to 3 minutes, until golden. Turn fillets over and cook for another 2 to 3 minutes.

TO SERVE Place a hot trout fillet on each individual plate. Serve with a wedge of lemon and a dollop of red pepper mayonnaise.

Serves 4

Taco Trout Bake

BRYAN SCHILLIE, Selwyn Lake Lodge, Saskatchewan

RAINBOW TROUT Farmed: *Best choice*;
Wild: *See Freshwater Fish, page 167*

Preheat the oven to 350°F or place a grill over a campfire. If you're cooking over a campfire, cut 4 sheets of aluminum foil, each 10 × 10 inches. (If you are cooking in the oven, try using parchment paper instead of foil.)

Place a trout fillet on the middle of each square of foil, shiny side out (or on parchment paper). Spread ¼ of the garlic and ¼ of the salsa over each fillet. Tightly fold one half of the foil (or parchment paper) over the trout, then fold the second half of the foil over the first. Tuck in the edges like an envelope so the trout is completely enclosed. If using an oven, place packages, seam side down, on a baking sheet. Bake (or grill) until fillets are fully cooked, 12 to 15 minutes. Remove from the oven (or grill) and carefully open the packets (the steam is very hot). Sprinkle fillets with cheddar cheese and green onions, then reseal the packages to allow the cheese to melt.

TO SERVE Serve hot in the foil (or parchment paper) with french fries, corn, and beans for a delicious treat!

Serves 4

4 skinless trout fillets (each 6 to 8 oz)

2 Tbsp chopped garlic

1 cup salsa

1 cup grated cheddar cheese

½ cup chopped green onions, white and green parts

Seared Rainbow Trout with Smoothed Cauliflower and Raisin-Caper Brown Butter Emulsion

JASON ROJAS, Manhattan Restaurant, Vancouver
First-place winner, SeaChoice Culinary Competition

RAINBOW TROUT Farmed: *Best choice;*
Wild: *See Freshwater Fish, page 167*

RICE AND CAULIFLOWER
1 cup wild rice

1 cup whipping cream

Pinch of nutmeg

½ head cauliflower, in florets

BROWN BUTTER EMULSION
1 cup whipping cream

2 Tbsp butter

Juice of 1 lemon

1 Tbsp golden raisins

1 Tbsp capers

RICE AND CAULIFLOWER In a small saucepan, bring 2 cups of salted water to a boil on high heat. Add wild rice, stir, cover, and reduce the heat to low. Cook rice until tender, about 40 minutes. Remove from the heat.

In another saucepan, bring cream to a gentle boil on medium heat. Stir in nutmeg and cauliflower, cover, and cook, stirring occasionally, until cauliflower is very tender and the liquid is reduced, 6 to 8 minutes. Cool slightly, then purée the cauliflower mixture in a blender. (You should have a thick purée. If it is too runny, place purée in a saucepan on medium heat until it thickens slightly.) Season with salt and pepper, then pour the purée back into the saucepan and cover to keep warm.

BROWN BUTTER EMULSION In a small saucepan, bring cream to a gentle boil on medium heat.

In a separate saucepan, heat butter on medium-high heat until it starts to turn brown. Whisking constantly, gradually pour the browned butter into the hot cream. Continue to whisk until the sauce is emulsified. Stir in lemon juice, raisins, and capers. Season with salt to taste, cover, and keep warm.

SEARED TROUT Season trout on both sides with salt and pepper. Heat canola oil in a frying pan on medium-high heat. Add trout and sear, skin side down, until golden brown, 2 to 3 minutes. Turn fillets over and cook for 1 minute more. Remove from the heat.

TO SERVE Spoon rice and cauliflower onto the centre of four plates. Top each serving with a fillet of trout and drizzle with the brown butter emulsion. Garnish with celery leaves.

Serves 4

SEARED TROUT

4 rainbow trout fillets
(each 4 to 6 oz), skin on

2 Tbsp canola oil

5 to 6 baby celery
leaves, for garnish

Cornmeal-crusted Rainbow Trout with Spot Prawn Salad and Garlic-Caper Butter

TERRY GERETA, Mise Restaurant, Winnipeg

RAINBOW TROUT Farmed: *Best choice;*
Wild: *See Freshwater Fish, page 167*

SPOT PRAWNS *Best choice*

GARLIC CONFIT
12 cloves garlic, peeled

1/3 cup olive oil

SPOT PRAWN SALAD
12 cups cold water

1 star anise

1/2 lemon, unpeeled and coarsely chopped

1/2 tsp fennel seeds

1/4 tsp salt

1/2 cup cold-pressed canola oil

2 ripe Roma tomatoes, seeded and sliced in thick strips

1 small red bell pepper, roasted, seeded, and diced

2 Tbsp chopped green onions, white and green parts

20 spot prawn tails

4 cups loosely packed fresh arugula

GARLIC CONFIT Place garlic in a small saucepan and cover with olive oil. Cook on low heat until cloves are soft, about 10 minutes. Strain oil through a fine-mesh sieve into an airtight container. Refrigerate immediately and use within 1 week. Reserve the garlic cloves and allow them to cool.

SPOT PRAWN SALAD In a large saucepan, combine water, star anise, lemon, fennel seeds, and salt. Bring to a boil on medium-high heat, then reduce the heat to low and simmer to draw out the flavours, about 30 minutes. Strain the mixture through a fine-mesh sieve and discard the solids. Return the infusion to the saucepan.

Preheat the oven to 200°F. In a metal bowl, combine canola oil, tomatoes, roasted red peppers, and green onions. Place in the oven to keep warm.

Bring the infusion to a simmer on medium heat. Add prawns and poach until just cooked, 3 to 4 minutes. Drain in a colander. Gently stir prawns into the tomato and pepper mixture. Add arugula and toss to mix. Allow to stand so that leaves wilt.

CORNMEAL-CRUSTED TROUT Spread cornmeal on a large plate. Season trout with salt and pepper, then cut each fillet in half crosswise. Dredge fillets in cornmeal, shaking off any excess.

Heat canola oil in a frying pan on medium-high heat. Add trout and pan-fry on one side for 3 to 4 minutes. Turn fillets over and pan-fry for another 3 to 4 minutes. Remove from the heat and transfer to a large plate.

Wipe out the frying pan with a crust of bread and discard. Add butter, capers, and garlic confit and cook on low heat until butter and garlic are brown, 3 to 5 minutes.

TO SERVE Arrange the salad on four plates. Top with a fillet of trout and spoon garlic-caper butter around the base of the salad. Serve immediately.

Serves 4 as a first course

CORNMEAL-
CRUSTED TROUT
½ cup cornmeal

2 trout fillets
(each 6 oz), skin on

2 Tbsp canola oil

3 Tbsp butter

1 tsp capers

Albacore Tuna Tacones with
Spicy Spot Prawn Mayonnaise

KUNAL GHOSE, Red Fish, Blue Fish, Victoria

TUNA Troll-caught: *Best choice*; US, pelagic long-line: *Some concerns*; Pacific, international, pelagic long-line: *Avoid*; Bluefin: *Avoid*

SPOT PRAWNS *Best choice*

MARINATED ONIONS
2 red onions, thinly sliced

4 Tbsp fresh lemon juice

4 Tbsp mirin
(Japanese rice wine)

SPICY PRAWN MAYONNAISE
2 Tbsp canola oil

½ lb spot prawn
tails, peeled

1 Tbsp sriracha (Thai hot sauce) or hot chili sauce

1 Tbsp fresh lime juice

1 Tbsp mirin

2 cups mayonnaise

MARINATED ONIONS Place onions in a small bowl. Stir in lemon juice and mirin and marinate for about 2 hours, or until ready to use.

SPICY PRAWN MAYONNAISE Coat a large frying pan with canola oil and set on high heat. Add prawns and stir-fry until cooked through, 1 to 2 minutes. Stir in sriracha (or chili sauce), lime juice, and mirin, then sprinkle with sea salt and cracked black pepper. Using a wooden spoon, scrape up any brown bits from the bottom of the pan and stir them into the cooking liquid.

Transfer the prawns and their cooking liquid to a food processor and purée until well mixed. Strain through a fine-mesh sieve into a bowl, discarding any solids. Allow to cool slightly, then beat in mayonnaise. Will keep refrigerated in an airtight container for up to 24 hours.

TACONES Lightly coat one side of each tortilla with about ⅛ tsp of the olive oil. In a small bowl, stir together sea salt, pepper, coriander, and cumin.

In another bowl, toss cabbage with pumpkin seeds. Stir in a quarter of the mixed spices.

Coat the tuna loin with 2 Tbsp of the olive oil. Sprinkle with the remaining mixed spices and rub them into the flesh.

Heat a frying pan on high heat or preheat a grill to high. Add tuna and sear for about 30 seconds. Turn loin over and sear for another 30 seconds. (Tuna is best served rare, so sear it as quickly as possible; remember, it will continue to cook a bit once you take it off the heat.) To test for doneness, cut into the tuna with a knife. The centre of the fish should be warm but not light in colour. Transfer to a cutting board.

Lightly brush one side of each tortilla with oil. Heat a large frying pan on high heat, then place a tortilla, oiled side down, in the pan and fry until golden, about 2 minutes. Transfer to a plate, and repeat with the remaining tortillas.

Cut tortillas in half. Position the tortilla halves with the straight edge on a 45-degree angle. Spread each tortilla with 1 Tbsp of the prawn mayonnaise. Thinly slice the tuna, placing three slices perpendicular to the straight edge in the middle of each tortilla. Divide the cabbage mixture, pea shoots, and marinated onions among the 10 tacones. Fold the point nearest you over the filling, so that the tip touches the curved edge of the tortilla and you end up with a horizontal fold in front of you. Then fold the top point toward you over the filling so that you end up with a cone-shaped wrap.

TO SERVE Serve immediately.

Makes 10 tacones

TACONES

5 flour tortillas (each 12-inch)

4 Tbsp olive oil, or more

1 Tbsp sea salt

1 Tbsp fresh cracked black pepper

1 Tbsp coriander seeds, roasted then ground

½ Tbsp cumin seeds, roasted then ground

1 small head cabbage, thinly sliced

½ cup pumpkin seeds, roasted then ground

¾ lb tuna loin

Small handful of pea shoots

Spice-seared Tuna with Avocado, Mango, and Pea Shoot Salad

JASON WILSON, Brix Restaurant and Wine Bar, Vancouver

TUNA Troll-caught: *Best choice*; US, pelagic long-line: *Some concerns*; Pacific, international, pelagic long-line: *Avoid*; Bluefin: *Avoid*

SPICE MIX
2 Tbsp coriander seeds

2 Tbsp sugar

1 tsp ground ginger

1 tsp black peppercorns

1 tsp crushed chili flakes

1 Tbsp fleur de sel

SEARED TUNA
12 oz tuna loin

2 ripe avocadoes

2 ripe mangoes

8 oz pea shoots

1 red bell pepper

1 bunch green onions

4 Tbsp fresh lime juice

2 tsp sesame oil

2 Tbsp light soy sauce

¼ tsp fresh pressed ginger

6 Tbsp rice bran oil
(or canola oil)

2 oz pickled ginger,
for garnish

SPICE MIX Place spice ingredients in a coffee grinder and grind thoroughly.

SEARED TUNA Place spice mix in a shallow bowl. Cut tuna into four equal portions, then dredge each piece liberally in the spice mix.

Heat 2 Tbsp of the rice bran oil (or canola oil) in a frying pan on medium-high heat. Add tuna and sear lightly on all sides (about 10 seconds per side). Remove from the heat and set aside.

Cut the avocado in half lengthwise, remove and discard the pit and slice into thin slices. Discard the peel. Peel the mango, then slice it thinly lengthwise. Discard the pit. Set aside.

In a small bowl, combine lime juice, sesame oil, soy sauce, ginger and the remaining rice bran oil (or canola oil) and whisk until well emulsified.

Slice green onions thinly at an angle and finely dice red bell pepper. Place pea shoots in a small bowl, add green onions, bell peppers and ¾ of the soy-ginger dressing. Toss until well combined.

TO SERVE Arrange alternating and overlapping slices of avocado and mango in a circle around four individual plates (use half an avocado and half a mango per plate). Place a mound of pea shoot salad in the middle of each avocado/mango ring. With a sharp knife, slice the tuna into thin, even pieces and fan 6 to 8 slices over each salad. Drizzle the remaining dressing over the mangoes and avocadoes. Garnish each serving with a quarter of the pickled ginger.

Serves 4

Sicilian-style Baked Albacore Tuna with Tomatoes, Green Olives, Capers, and Raisins

KAREN BARNABY, The Fish House in Stanley Park, Vancouver

TUNA Troll-caught: *Best choice*; US, pelagic long-line: *Some concerns*; Pacific, international, pelagic long-line: *Avoid*; Bluefin: *Avoid*

Preheat the oven to 450°F. In a large frying pan, heat olive oil on medium-high heat until hot but not smoking. Add tuna and sear lightly on one side for 2 to 3 minutes. Turn steaks over and sear for another 2 to 3 minutes. Remove from the heat, season both sides with sea salt and freshly ground black pepper, and transfer to a baking dish just large enough to hold the steaks.

In the pan used to sear the tuna, sauté onion and celery on medium heat until translucent, 4 to 5 minutes. Add tomatoes and reserved juice and pepper flakes. Simmer until the sauce begins to thicken, about 15 minutes. Stir in olives, capers, raisins, and basil. Taste and adjust the seasonings as needed. Spoon the sauce over the steaks, then bake on the centre rack for 10 to 15 minutes.

TO SERVE Place one tuna steak on each of four warmed plates. Spoon sauce over top and serve immediately.

Serves 4

4 Tbsp extra-virgin olive oil

4 albacore tuna steaks (each 6 oz)

1 cup finely diced onions

½ cup thinly sliced celery

1 can (28 oz) peeled Italian plum tomatoes, coarsely chopped and juice reserved

¼ tsp hot red pepper flakes

⅓ cup pitted green olives, cut in half

2 Tbsp capers

2 Tbsp golden raisins

¼ cup fresh basil leaves

Blackened Tuna with Baby Shrimp and Tomato Salsa

LESLEY STOWE, caterer and cracker maven, Vancouver

TUNA Troll-caught: *Best choice*; US, pelagic long-line: *Some concerns*; Pacific, international, pelagic long-line: *Avoid*; Bluefin: *Avoid*

SHRIMP Trap-caught: *Best choice*; Trawled: *Some concerns*; Warm-water: *Avoid*

BABY SHRIMP AND TOMATO SALSA

1 lb fresh hand-peeled baby shrimp

5 Roma tomatoes, seeded and diced

2 cloves garlic, crushed

3 Tbsp capers

4 Tbsp olive oil

3 Tbsp julienned basil leaves

BLACKENED TUNA

¼ cup unsalted butter, melted

¼ cup olive oil

1 tsp sea salt

1 Tbsp sweet paprika

1 tsp cayenne pepper

½ tsp white pepper

½ tsp black pepper

½ tsp chopped fresh thyme

½ tsp chopped fresh oregano

2 tsp vegetable oil

8 tuna steaks (each 8 oz)

BABY SHRIMP AND TOMATO SALSA In a bowl, toss shrimp with tomatoes, garlic, capers, olive oil, and basil. Season with sea salt to taste. Transfer to a small serving bowl and set aside. Will keep refrigerated in an airtight container for up to 24 hours.

BLACKENED TUNA In a bowl, combine butter and olive oil. In another bowl, mix sea salt, paprika, cayenne, white and black peppers, thyme, and oregano. Dip each tuna steak in the butter mixture, then lightly coat it in the spice mixture. The tuna doesn't have to be completely coated.

Turn on the stove exhaust fan to its highest setting. Heat a cast-iron frying pan on high heat until very hot, about 8 minutes. Carefully add a little vegetable oil to the hot pan. Add 4 of the steaks, making sure they don't touch each other. Sear on one side for 1 to 1½ minutes. Turn over and sear for another 1 to 1½ minutes. (Tuna is best served rare, so sear it as quickly as possible but keep an eye on the heat—you don't want to burn or overcook it. Remember, it will continue to cook a bit once you take it off the heat.) To test for doneness, cut into the tuna with a knife. The centre of the fish should be warm but not light in colour. Transfer the cooked steaks to a large platter. Sear the remaining 4 steaks.

TO SERVE Arrange the tuna steaks on the platter or serve them on individual plates. Spoon baby shrimp and tomato salsa over top.

Serves 8

Sesame-seared Albacore Tuna with Fennel and Microgreen Salad

ANDREA JEFFERSON, Quince, Vancouver

TUNA Troll-caught: *Best choice*; US, pelagic long-line: *Some concerns*; Pacific, international, pelagic long-line: *Avoid*; Bluefin: *Avoid*

SESAME-SEARED TUNA In a small bowl, combine white and black sesame seeds, cayenne, and salt. Spread this mixture on a plate. Press each tuna fillet into the spice mixture, coating both sides.

Turn on the stove exhaust fan to its highest setting. Heat vegetable oil in a large frying pan on high heat until it is almost smoking. Add the tuna fillets and sear on all sides, about 15 seconds per side. (Tuna is best served rare, so sear it as quickly as possible but keep an eye on the heat—you don't want to burn or overcook it. Remember, it will contiue to cook a bit once you take it off the heat.) To test for doneness, cut into the tuna with a knife. The centre of the fish should be warm but not light in colour. Remove from the heat and slice thinly.

FENNEL AND MICROGREEN SALAD In a large bowl, whisk together garlic, ginger, soy sauce, rice vinegar, and lime juice. Slowly whisk in sesame and grapeseed oils until well combined. Toss the microgreens in the dressing.

TO SERVE Divide the microgreen salad among four plates. Arrange the fennel and cucumber slices beside it. Fan four tuna slices on top of each salad.

Serves 4

SESAME-SEARED TUNA
- 2 Tbsp white sesame seeds
- 2 Tbsp black sesame seeds
- ¼ tsp cayenne pepper
- ½ tsp salt
- 4 skinless tuna fillets (each 5 oz)
- 2 Tbsp vegetable oil

FENNEL AND MICROGREEN SALAD
- 1 clove garlic, minced
- 1 tsp grated ginger
- ¼ cup soy sauce
- 1 Tbsp rice vinegar
- Juice of 1 lime
- 1 Tbsp sesame oil
- 1 Tbsp grapeseed oil
- 4 generous handfuls of microgreens
- 1 bulb fennel, thinly sliced
- 1 English cucumber, thinly sliced

Grilled Albacore Tuna with Fennel, Watercress, and Blood Orange Salad

ANGELO PROSPERI-PORTA, Cooper's Cove Guesthouse, Sooke, British Columbia

TUNA Troll-caught: *Best choice*; US, pelagic long-line: *Some concerns*; Pacific, international, pelagic long-line: *Avoid*; Bluefin: *Avoid*

FENNEL, WATERCRESS, AND BLOOD ORANGE SALAD

1 bulb fennel, tough root end and stalk removed

¼ cup + 1 Tbsp olive oil

1 bunch watercress, tough stems removed

4 blood oranges, peeled and white pith removed

1 Tbsp fresh lemon juice

FENNEL, WATERCRESS, AND BLOOD ORANGE SALAD Bring a large pot of salted water to a rapid boil on high heat. Using a sharp knife, cut fennel in quarters and add to the water. Reduce the heat to medium and simmer for 5 to 8 minutes, or until just tender. Drain well.

Heat a grill or a heavy-bottomed frying pan on medium-high heat. Lightly coat fennel with 1 Tbsp of the olive oil, then place on the grill or in the frying pan. Grill or sear, turning once, until fennel is lightly browned in spots, 3 to 4 minutes. Remove from the heat and set aside.

Cut watercress in 2-inch pieces and place in a bowl.

Set a fine-mesh sieve over a small bowl. Using a sharp knife and working over the sieve, cut out orange segments, making sure any juice flows through the sieve into the bowl. Add the orange segments to the watercress. Slice fennel across the grain in pieces ¼ inch thick, discarding any tough or stringy parts. Add fennel to the watercress and oranges.

In a small bowl, combine blood orange juice and lemon juice to taste. Whisk in the remaining olive oil and season with salt and pepper. Set aside until ready to serve.

GRILLED TUNA In a small bowl, combine honey and balsamic vinegar and set aside.

Rub tuna with olive oil, then season with salt and pepper. Heat a grill or a frying pan on medium-high heat. Add tuna and grill or sear for 1½ minutes. Grill or sear the remaining 3 sides for 1½ minutes each, or until rare. (Tuna is best served rare, so sear it as quickly as possible but keep an eye on the heat—you don't want to burn or overcook it. Remember, it will contiue to cook a bit once you take it off the heat.) To test for doneness, cut into the tuna with a knife. The centre of the fish should be warm but not light in colour. Remove from the heat and transfer to a platter. Brush tuna on all sides with the honey and balsamic vinegar mixture. Just before serving, cut in 12 slices.

TO SERVE Add half of the salad dressing to the salad and toss lightly to coat. Arrange the salad in the middle of a serving platter. Top with slices of tuna, then drizzle with the remaining dressing and serve immediately.

Serves 4 as a first course

GRILLED TUNA
1 Tbsp honey

1 Tbsp balsamic vinegar

1 sushi-grade albacore tuna loin (12 to 14 oz), trimmed to a uniform thickness

1 Tbsp extra-virgin olive oil

Walleye Fillets with St. Lawrence Crayfish, Summer Vegetable Medley, and Basil

ANNE DESJARDINS, L'Eau à la Bouche, Saint-Adèle, Quebec

WALLEYE See *Freshwater Fish*, page 167

CRAYFISH US, farmed: *Best choice*; International, farmed: *Avoid*; Wild: See *Freshwater Fish*, page 167

2 Tbsp + 1 tsp extra-virgin olive oil

2 cloves garlic, minced

4 green onions, white and green parts, minced

Zest and juice of 1 orange

¾ cup white vermouth

1¼ cups water

3 to 4 drops of Tabasco sauce

12 live crayfish

4 skinless walleye fillets (each 6 oz)

10 large fresh basil leaves, chopped

1 red bell pepper, seeded and finely diced

8 miniature pattypan squash, diced, or 1 zucchini, diced

Heat 1 tsp of the olive oil in a saucepan on medium heat. Add garlic, half the green onions, and half the orange zest. Stir in orange juice, vermouth, and water, then season with salt and Tabasco and bring to a boil.

Immerse crayfish in the boiling liquid. When they are just starting to turn red, after about 3 minutes, remove them from the pot. Do not overcook. Reduce the heat to a simmer.

Separate the tails from the crayfish bodies. Set aside the tails. Return the bodies to the poaching liquid in the pot and simmer until bouillon is reduced by half. Strain the bouillon through a fine-mesh sieve, discarding any solids, and set aside. Reserve 4 crayfish heads for garnish, discarding the remaining ones.

Preheat the oven to 150°F. Heat 1 Tbsp of the olive oil in a heavy-bottomed frying pan on medium heat. Add walleye fillets and cook for 2 to 3 minutes on each side, then transfer to an ovenproof dish. Season with salt and sprinkle with half of the basil and the remaining orange zest. Keep warm in the oven.

To the same frying pan, add the remaining olive oil. Add red peppers and squash (or zucchini), the remaining green onions, and the crayfish tails and sauté for 2 minutes on medium heat. Add to the walleye fillets in the oven.

Deglaze the frying pan with the crayfish bouillon. Simmer on low heat to reduce to a sauce consistency, about 3 minutes. Season with salt, Tabasco, and the remaining basil.

TO SERVE Divide the vegetables and crayfish among four warmed plates. Top with the walleye fillets, then pour sauce over each fillet, and garnish with a crayfish head.

Serves 4

Rocky Mountain Whitefish with Wilted Greens and Sauce Gribiche

DAVID WYSE, Quarry Bistro, Canmore, Alberta

ROCKY MOUNTAIN WHITEFISH *See Freshwater Fish, page 167*

SAUCE GRIBICHE
1 hard-cooked egg

1 green onion, white and green parts, thinly sliced

1 Tbsp finely chopped pickled beet

½ tsp grainy mustard

1 Tbsp rice vinegar

¼ cup canola oil, cold-pressed if possible

1 Tbsp finely chopped Italian flat-leaf parsley

PAN-FRIED WHITEFISH
4 fillets Rocky Mountain whitefish (each 6 oz), skin on, scaled

¼ tsp kosher salt

¼ tsp pepper

¼ cup all-purpose flour

¼ cup cornstarch

1 tsp crushed hot red pepper flakes

2 Tbsp unsalted butter

2 Tbsp extra-virgin olive oil

1 clove garlic, very thinly sliced

½ lemon

SAUCE GRIBICHE Peel the egg and, for the best texture, separate the white from the yolk. Discard the shell. Finely chop the white and the yolk and place them in a small bowl. Add green onions, pickled beets, grainy mustard, rice vinegar, canola oil, and parsley and mix until well combined. Season with salt and pepper. Will keep refrigerated in an airtight container for up to 24 hours.

PAN-FRIED WHITEFISH With a sharp knife, score each whitefish fillet 3 times, about ⅛ of an inch deep, on the skin side. Season fish with kosher salt and pepper.

In a shallow dish, combine flour, cornstarch, and red pepper flakes. Season with pinches of kosher salt and pepper. Dredge whitefish fillets in the flour mixture, making sure that both sides are well coated. Shake off any excess flour.

Heat butter and olive oil in a large frying pan on medium-high heat. When the butter just begins to brown, add the whitefish fillets, skin side down, and cook for about 4 minutes, or until the skin is brown and crispy. Carefully turn the fillets over and cook for another 4 minutes. Transfer to a plate and keep warm on the stove until ready to serve.

Add garlic to the frying pan and cook until lightly browned, about 3 minutes. Add a squeeze of lemon juice. Remove lemon butter sauce from the heat and set aside.

WILTED GREENS Heat butter and olive oil in a large frying pan on medium heat. Add beet greens and pea shoots, then increase the heat to medium-high and toss greens until they just begin to wilt. Season with salt and pepper.

TO SERVE Heat the lemon butter sauce on medium heat. Divide the wilted greens evenly among four plates, then top with a whitefish fillet. Spoon a tablespoon of the lemon butter sauce over each fillet and drizzle sauce gribiche around the edge of each plate.

Serves 4

WILTED GREENS

1 Tbsp unsalted butter

1 tsp extra-virgin olive oil

2 bunches beet greens, washed and trimmed

8 oz pea shoots (one whole clamshell container)

shellfish &

molluscs

Clam Miso Soup

GABRIELLE BRIGHT, *Canadian Living* magazine

CLAMS Farmed: *Best choice*; Atlantic, soft shell: *Some concerns*;
Atlantic, dredged: *Avoid*

In a large saucepan, bring clams, sake, lemon, and ginger to a boil on medium-high heat. Cover and steam until the clams open, about 5 minutes. Discard any clams that do not open. Remove from the heat and set aside.

In a separate saucepan, bring 2 cups water to a boil on high heat. In a small bowl, whisk miso paste with 1 additional cup cold water until smooth, then add this miso broth to the boiling water.

TO SERVE Divide clams, lemons, ginger, and cooking liquid evenly among four bowls. Pour a quarter of the miso mixture over each serving. Sprinkle with green onions and serve.

Serves 4

20 littleneck or Manila clams

⅓ cup sake (Japanese rice wine)

4 thin slices lemon

4 thin slices fresh ginger

3 Tbsp white miso paste (available at Asian food stores and many supermarkets)

2 green onions, white and green parts, thinly sliced on the diagonal, for garnish

Maritime Clam Chowder

MICHAEL SMITH, cookbook author and television host,
Fortune, Prince Edward Island

CLAMS Farmed: *Best choice*; Atlantic, soft shell: *Some concerns*;
Atlantic, dredged: *Avoid*

4 slices bacon, chopped

1 onion, peeled and coarsely chopped

2 stalks celery, coarsely chopped

¼ cup white wine

1 cup whipping cream

1 cup milk

2 cans (each 5 oz) clam meat

1 large baking potato, unpeeled, coarsely grated

2 bay leaves

3 to 4 sprigs fresh thyme, leaves only

1 can (12 oz) evaporated milk (*not* sweetened condensed milk)

½ cup fresh Italian flat-leaf parsley leaves

In a large heavy-bottomed stockpot, combine bacon and a splash of water. Heat on medium-high heat, stirring, until bacon crisps, about 7 minutes. Pour off most of the fat.

Deglaze the pot with another splash of water, loosening any browned bits on the bottom. Add onions and celery and sauté for 2 to 3 minutes, or until they soften and smell fragrant. Stir in white wine, cream, milk, and clam meat, then add potato, bay leaves, and thyme. Bring to a slow simmer, stirring frequently. Reduce the heat to medium and simmer until the potato softens, releasing its starches and thickening the chowder, about 20 minutes.

Add evaporated milk and cook, stirring frequently, until the chowder is heated through. Season with salt and pepper, then stir in parsley.

TO SERVE Ladle chowder into bowls, being sure to divide the clam meat evenly, and serve immediately with your favourite biscuits.

Serves 4 to 6

Clam Rarebit

FRÉDÉRIC MORIN, Liverpool House and Joe Beef, Montreal

CLAMS Farmed: *Best choice*; Atlantic, soft shell: *Some concerns*; Atlantic, dredged: *Avoid*

Bring beer to a boil in a saucepan on medium-high heat. Add clams, cover, and steam until they are just open, about 5 minutes. Discard any clams that do not open. Using a slotted spoon, transfer clams to a bowl and allow to cool. Reserve the cooking liquid.

Line a plate with a paper bag. In a frying pan on medium heat, cook bacon until crisp, about 5 minutes. Drain bacon on the paper bag–lined plate. Crumble bacon and set aside.

In a food processor, pulse 2 slices of the toast until they become coarse crumbs. Set aside. Remove clams from the shells and chop coarsely.

Preheat the oven to 400°F. In a large bowl, combine clams, bacon, bread crumbs, shallots, chives, and cream cheese. If the mixture is too thick to spread, add clam cooking liquid 1 tsp at a time. Spread each of the 2 remaining slices of toast with half of the clam mixture. Top each sandwich with half the cheddar and half the butter. Place sandwiches on a baking sheet and bake until the cheese melts and the clam mixture is golden brown, 5 to 8 minutes.

TO SERVE Place one clam rarebit on each warmed plate. Serve with a cold spicy Caesar.

Serves 2

¼ cup beer

16 littleneck clams (about ½ lb total weight)

2 slices bacon, diced

4 slices fine white bread, such as Pullman or brioche, toasted and crusts removed

¼ tsp chopped shallots

¼ tsp minced chives

2 Tbsp cream cheese

¼ cup grated cheddar cheese

1 tsp butter, in small pieces

Shaved Geoduck Salad
with Sesame-Soy Vinaigrette

ANDREA JEFFERSON, Quince, Vancouver

GEODUCK CLAMS *Some concerns*

1 small geoduck
clam (1 to 2 lbs)

2 Tbsp rice vinegar

1 Tbsp soy sauce

2 tsp grated ginger

2 Tbsp sesame oil

2/3 English cucumber,
thinly sliced

1½ cups bean sprouts,
washed, for garnish

2 Tbsp sesame seeds,
toasted, for garnish

2 green onions, white and
green parts, finely sliced on
the diagonal, for garnish

Fill a large bowl with ice water. Bring a large pot of water to a boil on high heat. Drop geoduck into the boiling water and blanch for 30 seconds. Using a slotted spoon, transfer geoduck to the bowl of ice water for 30 seconds. Using a flexible paring knife, pry open the shell, then cut the siphon (the long neck) from the body of the clam and set aside. (If the shell does not open easily, blanch geoduck for another 10 seconds, then shock in the ice water and try again.)

You can remove the brown belly meat and reserve it for another use, but remove and discard the intestines, which are the dark, egg-sized, oval mass, carefully cutting around them and trimming any attached membranes. (Refrigerate the brown belly meat in an airtight container and use it within 24 hours for soups or other dishes that call for littleneck clams or butter clams, or freeze it for up to one month.)

With the back of a knife, rub the skin on the siphon to loosen it, then peel it off as though removing a rubber glove. Discard the skin. Place siphon in the freezer for 10 minutes. (This firms it up and makes it easier to slice.)

While the siphon is in the freezer, make the vinaigrette. In a small bowl, whisk together rice vinegar and soy sauce. Squeeze the grated ginger with your fingertips to extract the ginger juice and add the juice to the vinaigrette. Discard the solid ginger. Whisking constantly, slowly pour sesame oil into the vinaigrette until the mixture is well emulsified.

Remove siphon from the freezer and slice as thinly as possible into rings. The slices should be translucent and very fine.

TO SERVE Divide cucumber evenly among the plates. Top with shaved geoduck, then drizzle with vinaigrette. Garnish each plate with bean sprouts, sesame seeds, and green onions.

Serves 4 as a first course

Geoduck with Wild Nodding Onion
and Hazelnut Butter Sauce

SINCLAIR PHILIP, Sooke Harbour House, Sooke, British Columbia

GEODUCK CLAMS *Some concerns*

1 geoduck clam (1 to 2 lbs)

¼ cup dry Riesling or other dry white wine

½ cup fish stock (page 21)

2 wild nodding onions, green parts only, or chives, in 3-inch lengths + 1 tsp finely chopped

2 garlic chives, in 3-inch lengths + 1 tsp finely chopped

20 whole hazelnuts, toasted

1 tsp apple cider vinegar

½ cup unsalted butter, cold and cubed

3 Tbsp vegetable oil

2 thin slices red onion

2 thin slices Walla Walla onion

1 small leek, white part only, thinly sliced

1 shallot, in quarters

2 to 4 wild nodding onion blossoms, for garnish

2 to 4 garlic chive blossoms, for garnish

Fill a large bowl with cold water. Rinse geoduck under very hot tap water for about 1 minute to loosen the skin, then submerge in the cold water. Insert a flexible paring knife between the shell and the body of the geoduck around the base of the siphon (the long neck), then cut along the edge of the shell to separate the shell from the body. Gently pull the shell away from the body. With the back of a knife, rub the skin on the siphon to loosen it, then peel it off as though removing a rubber glove. Discard the skin. Slice siphon as thinly as possible into rings. Set aside.

Remove and discard the intestines, which are the dark, egg-sized, oval mass, carefully cutting around them and trimming any attached membranes. (You can refrigerate the brown belly meat in an airtight container and use it within 24 hours for soups or other dishes that call for littleneck clams or butter clams, or freeze it up to one month.)

In a large saucepan on high heat, boil white wine and fish stock until reduced to ¼ cup, 10 to 12 minutes. Add the 1 tsp of nodding onion greens (or chives), the 1 tsp of garlic chives, and hazelnuts. Return to a boil, then whisk in apple cider vinegar and butter until completely incorporated. Remove the sauce from the heat and set aside in a warm place.

Heat vegetable oil in a cast-iron frying pan on high heat. When the pan starts to smoke, add red and Walla Walla onions, leeks, the remaining nodding onion greens (or chives), the remaining garlic chives, and shallots. Sauté for 1 minute. Add sliced geoduck and sauté for 30 seconds more, just enough to warm it through. (Be very careful not to overcook the geoduck or it will be tough.)

TO SERVE Divide the onion hazelnut sauce between two plates. Top with the geoduck mixture. Garnish the edges of the plates with wild nodding onion blossoms, then sprinkle with garlic chive blossoms.

Serves 2

Gingered Cantaloupe Soup
with Spiced Crab and Spot Prawns

LIANA ROBBERECHT, Calgary Petroleum Club, Calgary

DUNGENESS CRAB *Best choice*

SPOT PRAWNS *Best choice*

2 ripe cantaloupes, peeled, seeded, and roughly chopped

2 tsp olive oil

½ tsp grated lemon grass (available at Asian food markets)

2 Tbsp grated fresh ginger

1 Tbsp minced shallots

½ cup fish stock (page 21) or chicken stock

¼ cup + 1 Tbsp sake (Japanese rice wine)

18 spot prawn tails, peeled

1 lb Dungeness crabmeat, cooked and picked over for cartilage

3 green onions, green part only, finely chopped

¼ tsp sambal oelek or hot chili sauce

In a food processor or a blender, purée cantaloupe until smooth, 30 to 45 seconds. Set aside.

Heat 1 tsp of the olive oil in a saucepan on medium heat. Add lemon grass, ginger, and half of the shallots and sauté for about 1 minute. Stir in fish (or chicken) stock and bring to a boil, then reduce the heat to medium-low and simmer for 1 hour.

Strain the stock through a fine-mesh sieve and discard any solids. Return the stock to the saucepan, add the cantaloupe purée and the ¼ cup of sake, and reduce for 30 minutes on low heat. Season with salt and pepper, being careful not to add too much salt. (The crabmeat is salty.) Cover with a lid and keep warm on low heat.

Heat a frying pan on medium heat. Add the remaining olive oil and shallots and sauté for 1 minute. Stir in spot prawns and the remaining sake and sauté until spot prawns are just cooked, 1 to 2 minutes. Add crabmeat and toss gently to warm through, then remove from the heat.

In a small bowl, gently combine green onions, sambal oelek (or chili sauce), and the seafood mixture.

TO SERVE Ladle hot cantaloupe soup into individual bowls. Spoon one-sixth of the seafood mixture into the middle of each bowl, then serve and enjoy immediately.

Serves 6

Creamed Corn and Dungeness Crab

VITALY PALEY, Paley's Place, Portland, Oregon

DUNGENESS CRAB *Best choice*

SWEET CORN STOCK Place corn cobs and onions in a large stockpot. Cover with water and bring to a boil on high heat. Reduce the heat to medium-low, then simmer for 30 minutes. If the stock has a sweet flavour, remove it from the heat; if not, simmer about 15 minutes more. Strain stock through a fine-mesh sieve, discarding any solids. You should have about 1 quart. Measure out ½ cup and set aside. The remaining stock will keep refrigerated in an airtight container up to 1 week or frozen for up to 1 month.

CREAMED CORN Place corn kernels in a large frying pan. Add enough corn stock to just cover the kernels, then cook gently on medium-high heat for 5 to 7 minutes. When the liquid has nearly all reduced, add crème fraîche and vanilla seeds. Simmer for 2 minutes more, then add crabmeat and orange zest. Season with salt and black pepper.

TO SERVE Transfer to a large serving bowl and serve immediately.

Serves 4

SWEET CORN STOCK
8 small (or 4 large) cobs sweet corn, kernels removed but reserved

1 Walla Walla onion, peeled and roughly chopped

CREAMED CORN
kernels from 8 small (or 4 large) cobs sweet corn

½ cup sweet corn stock, or more

1 cup crème fraîche

¼ vanilla bean, split and scraped, seeds only

4 to 6 oz Dungeness crabmeat, cooked and picked over for cartilage

Zest of 1 large orange

Ras-el Hanout Crab Salad with Onion Rings

VIKRAM VIJ, Vij's Restaurant, Vancouver

DUNGENESS CRAB *Best choice;*
Alaskan king, snow: *Some concerns*; Russian king: *Avoid*

CRAB SALAD
5 cups water

2 Tbsp ras-el hanout spice, whole, not ground (available at specialty food stores or online)

¼ tsp turmeric

½ tsp salt

1 lb crabmeat, picked over for cartilage

1¼ cups coconut cream

1 Tbsp finely chopped cilantro

1 Tbsp finely chopped jalapeño peppers, including seeds

1 Tbsp fresh lemon juice

CRAB SALAD Pour water into a large stockpot. Stir in ras-el hanout spice, turmeric, and salt. Simmer on medium heat until flavours from the spices are released, about 30 minutes. Reduce the heat to low so braising liquid is barely simmering.

Cut a piece of cheesecloth to 15 × 15 inches. Place crabmeat in the middle of the cheesecloth, bring the edges of the cheesecloth together and tie with string. (It is important to tie the sachet tightly so that the crabmeat won't escape, but leave enough room for the flavours in the water to flow around and penetrate the crabmeat.)

Add the crab sachet to the braising liquid and cook uncovered for 3 to 4 hours. Transfer the crab sachet to a colander and allow it to drain for 10 to 15 minutes. Discard the braising liquid.

Unwrap crab and place it in a stainless steel bowl. Add coconut cream, cilantro, and jalapeño to taste. Using a spatula, gently combine until well mixed, being careful not to crush or press hard or the crab will break apart. Season with salt, if needed. Refrigerate up to 3 hours.

ONION RINGS Line a large plate with a paper bag and set aside. Thinly slice onions into rounds and separate. Place egg in a shallow bowl. Fill a second shallow bowl with the flour. Dip onion rings into egg, then dredge with flour and shake off any excess. Repeat until all of the onions are coated.

Heat ¼ inch of vegetable oil in a small frying pan on high heat. Add onion rings in batches, being careful not to crowd the pan. Fry until golden and crispy, 2 to 3 minutes, turning the rings as necessary so they don't burn. Using a slotted spoon, transfer to the paper bag–lined plate to drain. Lightly sprinkle with salt.

TO SERVE Place one to two tablespoons of the crab salad into twelve small spoons (Chinese soup spoons work well), arranging the spoons on a serving tray. Drizzle each spoonful with a drop or two of lemon juice and garnish with onion rings.

Serves 6 as a first course

ONION RINGS
1 large onion

1 egg, beaten

¼ cup all-purpose flour

2 Tbsp vegetable oil, or more

Crispy Crab Cakes with Corn Salsa

MARINO TAVARES, Ferreira Café, Montreal

DUNGENESS CRAB *Best choice*

CORN SALSA
1 lb frozen corn kernels

1 small red onion,
finely chopped

1 clove garlic, finely chopped

3 Tbsp fresh Italian
flat-leaf parsley

3 Tbsp chopped
fresh cilantro

4 Tbsp olive oil

1 Tbsp red wine vinegar

Tabasco sauce to taste

CRAB CAKES
2 red bell peppers,
seeded and cut in quarters

2 lbs Dungeness crabmeat,
cooked and picked over
for cartilage

1 small onion, finely chopped

1 clove garlic, minced

2 Tbsp chopped
fresh cilantro

4 Tbsp mayonnaise

Tabasco sauce to taste

1 cup all-purpose flour

2 cups panko
(Japanese bread crumbs)

2 eggs, lightly beaten

¼ cup canola oil

1 tsp butter

CORN SALSA Bring a pot of salted water to a boil on high heat. Cook corn until tender, then drain, transfer to a medium bowl, and allow to cool in the refrigerator.

When the corn is cool, add red onions, garlic, parsley, cilantro, olive oil, and red wine vinegar to the bowl, stirring until well combined. Season to taste with Tabasco and salt. Will keep refrigerated in an airtight container for up to 24 hours.

CRAB CAKES Fill a large bowl with ice water. Bring a pot of water to a boil on high heat. Add red peppers and blanch for 1 minute. Using a slotted spoon, transfer red peppers to the bowl of ice water and allow to cool.

Line a baking sheet with parchment paper. In a food processor, pulse red peppers until chunky. Transfer to a large bowl, then add crabmeat, onions, garlic, cilantro, and mayonnaise. Season to taste with Tabasco and salt. Using a spoon, form the crab mixture into 12 patties, each about 2 inches in diameter, and place them on the lined baking sheet. Refrigerate for 1 to 2 hours.

Preheat the oven to 350°F. Place flour and panko on individual plates. Pour eggs into a shallow bowl. Dredge each patty in flour, then dip into the eggs and coat with panko. Set aside on the baking sheet.

Line a large ovenproof plate with a clean tea
towel. In a large cast-iron frying pan, heat oil and
butter on medium heat. Add patties and fry for
2 to 3 minutes, or until golden. Turn patties over
and pan-fry for another 2 to 3 minutes. Transfer
to the lined plate, and cook in the oven for about
5 minutes, or until warmed through.

TO SERVE Place one hot crab cake on each
warmed plate. Serve with one or two spoonfuls
of corn salsa.

Serves 12 as a first course

Dungeness Crab Cake Benedicts
with Chive Hollandaise Sauce

LYNN CRAWFORD, Four Seasons Hotel, New York

DUNGENESS CRAB *Best choice*

CHIVE HOLLANDAISE SAUCE

3 egg yolks

½ tsp hot sauce

½ tsp Worcestershire sauce

Juice of 1 lemon

⅛ cup melted butter

1 Tbsp finely chopped chives

CRAB CAKES

3 egg yolks, lightly beaten

2 tsp Dijon mustard

1 tsp Worcestershire sauce

Dash of hot sauce

1 lb Dungeness crabmeat, picked over for cartilage

1 green onion, green part only, finely chopped

½ cup mixed chopped fresh herbs, such as tarragon, parsley, and chives

½ cup panko (Japanese bread crumbs)

2 Tbsp vegetable oil

CHIVE HOLLANDAISE SAUCE In a bowl, whisk egg yolks until foamy, about 1 minute. Continue whisking while adding hot sauce, Worcestershire sauce, and lemon juice. Transfer the mixture to the top of a double boiler on medium heat. Continue whisking until the sauce thickens and forms ribbons when the whisk is lifted, 5 to 7 minutes. Remove the sauce from the heat and gently whisk in butter and chives. Season with salt and white pepper. Cover to keep warm.

CRAB CAKES In a mixing bowl, whisk egg yolks with Dijon mustard, Worcestershire sauce, and hot sauce. Stir in crabmeat, green onions, and mixed herbs. Season with pinches of salt and cracked black pepper. Add ¼ cup of the panko, then gradually add the remaining panko 1 Tbsp at a time until the mixture just binds together. Using a spoon, form the mixture into 8 crab cakes.

Preheat the oven to 325°F. Heat vegetable oil in a large frying pan on medium-high heat. Add crab cakes and sear until golden, about 2 minutes. Turn crab cakes over and sear another 2 minutes. Transfer crab cakes to a baking sheet and place in the oven to keep warm.

POACHED EGGS Bring a large saucepan of water to a simmer on medium heat. Stir in white vinegar, then gently crack in eggs. Do not allow water to boil, or the eggs will fall apart. Cook until the whites are opaque but yolks are still soft, about 5 minutes.

TO SERVE While the eggs are poaching, place two crab cakes on each plate. Using a slotted spoon, gently lift the eggs out of the water, allowing all of the water to drain off (otherwise the dish will become soggy). Season with salt and freshly ground black pepper. Place the eggs on the crab cakes and spoon chive hollandaise sauce over the eggs.

Serves 4

POACHED EGGS
½ cup white vinegar

8 eggs

Wokked Spiny Lobster

PATRICK LIN, Senses Restaurant, Toronto

SPINY LOBSTERS US, Australia, Western Baja: *Best choice*; International: *Avoid*

LOBSTER

4 spiny lobsters
(each about 1½ lbs)

1 onion, coarsely chopped

1 bay leaf

½ lemon

½ carrot

½ stalk celery

LOBSTER Fill a large bowl with ice water. Fill a pot large enough to hold all the lobsters with water. Add onions, bay leaf, lemon, carrot, celery, and pinches of sea salt to the pot. Cover with a lid and bring to a boil on high heat. Immerse lobsters and boil for 2 minutes.

Leaving the pot of boiling water on the heat, use tongs to transfer lobsters to the bowl of ice water. Once lobsters are cool enough to handle, about 15 minutes, place on a cutting board. Using a sharp knife, remove claws and knuckles and return them to the boiling water for 4 more minutes. Using tongs, transfer claws and knuckles to the ice water to cool.

Using a sharp knife, cut lobster tails in half and remove the meat. Roughly chop the meat from each tail into 8 to 10 pieces. Set aside.

Preheat the oven to 350°F. Clean out lobster bodies, discarding the rest of the innards. Arrange 4 half shells on a baking sheet and cook in the oven for 8 minutes. Remove and set aside.

Remove the claws and knuckles from the ice water. Using the tip of a knife or a lobster pick, extract the claw meat and reserve it in a small bowl. Repeat with the knuckle meat, reserving it in a second bowl.

GARNISH Reduce the oven heat to 325°F. In a frying pan, heat 1 tsp of the vegetable oil on medium heat. Add onions, bell peppers, and lobster tail and knuckle meat. Season with salt and pepper. Cook, stirring often, until onions are translucent, about 3 minutes. Remove from the heat.

Measure brandy (or cognac) into a measuring cup. (Pouring directly from the bottle into a hot pan can cause the vapours to lead back into the bottle and build enough pressure for the bottle to explode.) Pour brandy (or cognac) into the lobster mixture and return the pan to the heat. Once brandy (or cognac) is added, stand away from the stove and use a barbecue lighter or a long fireplace match to light the fumes of the alcohol at the edge of the pan. (Be careful to keep your hair and any loose clothing away from the pan, as the flames will rush up.) Allow the flames to burn for 1 minute or so; if they haven't subsided, cover the pan with a lid until the flames are out.

Spoon the flambéed mixture into the lobster shells, place them on a baking sheet and keep warm in the oven. Heat the remaining oil in the frying pan on medium heat. Add shallots, garlic, ginger, chili peppers, and claw meat and stir until warm, 1 to 2 minutes.

TO SERVE Arrange a lobster shell on individual warmed plates. Garnish each serving with a quarter of the lobster claw mixture and serve immediately.

Serves 4

GARNISH

2 tsp vegetable oil

½ onion, minced

2 Tbsp finely diced green bell pepper

2 Tbsp finely diced yellow bell pepper

2 Tbsp finely diced orange bell pepper

2 Tbsp brandy or cognac

2 small shallots, minced

2 cloves garlic, minced

1 Tbsp grated fresh ginger

½ tsp seeded and minced hot red chili peppers

Naked Lobster with Green Pea Purée and Sour Cream Mashed Potatoes

CHRIS AERNI, The Rossmount Inn, St. Andrews, New Brunswick

LOBSTER Atlantic Canada: *Best choice*; Atlantic US: *Some concerns*; Rock, spiny, US, Australia, Western Baja: *Best choice*; Spiny, international: *Avoid*

GREEN PEA PURÉE
½ cup fresh or frozen green peas

⅛ tsp granulated sugar

⅛ tsp salt

SOUR CREAM MASHED POTATOES
5 large Russet potatoes, peeled and cut in half

¼ cup milk

2 Tbsp butter

4 to 6 Tbsp sour cream

⅛ tsp ground nutmeg

½ tsp salt

½ tsp white pepper

1 Tbsp finely chopped chives

1 tsp white truffle oil (optional)

GREEN PEA PURÉE Bring 2 cups water to a boil in a medium saucepan on high heat. Add peas and boil until just cooked through, 1 to 2 minutes for fresh peas, 3 to 4 minutes for frozen. Remove from the heat and drain well.

Transfer peas to a food processor and purée until completely smooth. Strain through a fine-mesh sieve back into the saucepan, discarding any solids, and season to taste with sugar and salt. Cover and keep warm at the back of the stove.

SOUR CREAM MASHED POTATOES Bring a large pot of water to a boil on high heat. Add potatoes, reduce the heat to medium-high and cook potatoes until completely soft, about 12 minutes. Drain well and mash until smooth.

Using a whisk, beat in milk, butter, and sour cream until the mixture is light and airy. Season with nutmeg, salt, and white pepper. Cover pot with a lid, and keep warm at the back of the stove.

LOBSTER Fill a pot large enough to hold all the lobsters with water. Add cloves, onions, bay leaf, white vinegar, and sea salt. Bring to a boil on high

heat, add lobsters, then cover with a lid and bring back to a boil. Once the water is boiling, remove the pot from the heat. Allow to stand, covered, for 5 minutes.

Using tongs, transfer lobsters to a cutting board. Allow to cool. Working with one at a time and using a sharp knife, cut lobsters in half lengthwise. Remove tail meat from the shell. Using a nutcracker, crack claws and knuckles and remove the meat. Place lobster meat in a colander and rinse under cold running water. Reserve lobster shells to make stock or soup.

In a medium saucepan, melt butter on medium heat. Stir in vanilla bean, then add lobster meat. Reduce the heat to low and simmer, stirring often, just until lobster is reheated. (It is important not to overcook the lobster or it will be tough.)

TO SERVE Stir the chives and truffle oil, if using, into the mashed potatoes, then place two spoonfuls of potatoes in the centre of each plate. Arrange half a lobster tail, a claw, and some knuckle meat on top of the mashed potatoes. Spoon lobster butter over top. Drizzle pea purée around the plate and season with a dash of salt and pepper.

Serves 6

LOBSTER

3 whole cloves

1 large onion, cut in half

1 bay leaf

1/2 cup white vinegar

1/2 cup sea salt

3 Bay of Fundy lobsters (each about 2 lbs)

1 cup butter

1 vanilla bean, split in half

Bisque Mussels

GARNER QUAIN, Flex Mussels, Charlottetown

MUSSELS Farmed: *Best choice*; Wild: *Some concerns*

LOBSTER Atlantic Canada: *Best choice*; Atlantic US: *Some concerns*; Rock, spiny, US, Australia, Western Baja: *Best choice*; Spiny, international: *Avoid*

1 tsp extra-virgin olive oil

1 tsp fresh chopped garlic

2 green onions, white and green parts, chopped

1 tomato, coarsely chopped

4 oz lobster meat (tail and claw meat only), cooked and minced

¼ cup white wine

⅛ cup brandy

½ cup whipping cream

2¼ lbs mussels, cleaned and beards snipped off

2 sprigs fresh thyme, whole

½ lemon

NOTE The key to making great mussels is speed. Using high heat and a short cooking time, you can prevent overcooking. Have all of your ingredients ready and don't overload a pot with mussels. If you do not have a large pot, cook the mussels in smaller batches.

Heat olive oil in a large (16- to 20-cup) heavy-bottomed saucepan on medium-high heat. Add garlic, green onions, tomato, and lobster meat and sauté for 1 to 2 minutes, stirring frequently, until tomatoes begin to break down. Stir in white wine, brandy, and cream, gently scraping the bottom of the pot with a wooden spoon, and cook for 1 minute.

Add mussels and thyme. Cover with a tight-fitting lid and boil for 4 to 6 minutes, stirring gently just once, until all the mussels have opened wide. Using a slotted spoon, transfer mussels to a serving dish. Discard any unopened mussels. Squeeze lemon juice over the shellfish.

Reduce the sauce by one-third, 2 to 3 minutes, or until desired consistency is reached.

TO SERVE Pour the sauce over the mussels and serve immediately with plenty of baguette slices.

Serves 4 as a first course

Mussels and Clams Steamed
in an Asian-spiced Coconut Sauce

LEIF KRAVIS, Monsoon Restaurant, Toronto

MUSSELS AND CLAMS Farmed: *Best choice*; Wild: *Some concerns*

Heat a wok or a large cast-iron skillet on high heat and add canola oil. When the oil begins to smoke, add ginger, garlic, onions, chili peppers, and sugar. Stir constantly until the ingredients start to brown, about 2 minutes. Add lemon grass and sauté for another 2 minutes. Add tomatoes, coconut milk, lime juice, and fish sauce, stir well and bring to a boil, about 2 minutes.

Add clams and stir well. When the clams start to open, 6 to 8 minutes, add mussels and continue to stir. Cook until all the shellfish are open, 4 to 5 minutes. Discard any that do not open. The sauce should be reduced to a soup consistency. Season with salt and pepper. Add cilantro, reserving a few leaves for garnish, and stir well.

TO SERVE Divide the mussels and clams among four bowls, arranging them nicely. Pour the sauce over the shellfish and garnish each serving with a wedge of lime and some cilantro leaves. The aroma of the cilantro in the steam will be the first thing your guests notice as the bowls are placed in front of them. Serve with slices of warm baguette to soak up the sauce.

Serves 4

2 Tbsp canola oil

1 piece fresh ginger, about 1 inch, peeled, then finely minced or grated

4 cloves garlic, finely minced

1 large onion, finely diced

2 hot red chili peppers, thinly sliced

3 tsp granulated sugar

2 stems lemon grass, finely chopped (available at Asian food markets)

2 tomatoes, diced

1 can (14 oz) coconut milk

Juice of 2 limes

4 Tbsp fish sauce

1 lb Manila clams, well washed

2 lbs mussels, cleaned and beards snipped off

1 cup fresh cilantro leaves, well washed and loosely packed

1 lime, in 4 to 8 wedges, for garnish

Drunken Mussels

HIDEKAZU TOJO, Tojo's Restaurant, Vancouver

MUSSELS Farmed: *Best choice;* Wild: *Some concerns*

2 lbs mussels, cleaned and beards snipped off

½ cup sake (Japanese rice wine)

½ cup rice vinegar

1 Tbsp light soy sauce

1 Tbsp granulated sugar

1 Tbsp olive oil

10 button mushrooms, in half

1 Japanese cucumber, thinly sliced

½ onion, thinly sliced

Place mussels in a large deep saucepan on medium-high heat. Pour in sake and boil gently until mussels open, 6 to 8 minutes. Discard any mussels that do not open. Using a slotted spoon, scoop the mussels into a large bowl and refrigerate.

Gently boil the mussel poaching liquid on medium heat until reduced by half, 5 to 7 minutes. Stir in rice vinegar, soy sauce, sugar, olive oil, mushrooms, cucumbers, and onions. Transfer this sauce to a bowl and refrigerate until cold, about 1 hour.

Pour the sauce over the mussels and refrigerate to allow flavours to blend, about 4 hours. Drain the mussels and vegetables using a fine-mesh sieve and discard the marinade.

TO SERVE Arrange the mussels and vegetables on a platter. Pass around plates and have guests help themselves.

Serves 4 as a first course

Grilled Octopus Salad

NICK NUTTING, Pointe Restaurant, Tofino, British Columbia

OCTOPUS British Columbia: *Best choice*; US: *Some concerns*

Preheat the oven to 250°F. Bring a large pot of water to a boil on high heat. Add octopus and cook for 10 minutes. Drain octopus in a large colander.

In a large ovenproof pot with a lid, heat 2 tsp of the olive oil on medium-low heat. Add onions, fennel, garlic, hot pepper flakes, and fennel seeds and sauté for 2 to 3 minutes, until onions are translucent. Add white wine, capers, tomato juice, orange juice and zest, bay leaf, thyme, rosemary, basil, and the wine cork and stir to mix well. Add octopus, reduce the heat to medium, and bring to a simmer. Cover the pot and cook in the oven for about 3½ hours, or until octopus is tender. Remove from the heat and allow to cool slightly, then cover and refrigerate the octopus, in the braising liquid, overnight.

Preheat a barbecue or a grill on high heat. Remove octopus from the braising liquid and pat dry with an old tea towel. Place octopus on a cutting board. Using a sharp knife, trim off any excess purple skin and remove the suction cups from the tentacles. Discard these trimmings and the braising liquid.

continued overleaf . . .

4 to 6 lbs octopus (body and tentacles), fresh or defrosted if frozen

½ cup + 2 Tbsp + 2 tsp olive oil

1 onion, diced

1 bulb fennel, diced

1 head garlic, chopped

¼ tsp hot red pepper flakes

¼ tsp fennel seeds

¼ cup dry white wine

2 Tbsp capers

8 cups tomato juice

Zest and juice of 1 orange

1 bay leaf

2 sprigs fresh thyme, whole

2 sprigs fresh rosemary, whole

2 sprigs fresh basil, whole

1 wine cork

4 to 5 slices sourdough bread or focaccia

2 Tbsp fresh lemon juice

3 to 4 large bunches arugula, washed and torn into bite-sized pieces

½ cup niçoise olives, pitted

¼ cup balsamic vinegar

Place octopus directly on the barbecue (or grill) and sear on all sides, just long enough to put grill marks on the octopus, about 5 minutes per side. Remove from the heat and set aside to cool slightly. Leave the barbecue (or grill) on.

Brush bread slices with 2 Tbsp of the olive oil, then toast on the barbecue (or grill) for about 2 minutes. Turn bread over and cook for another 2 minutes, or until golden. Transfer bread to a cutting board and chop into ½-inch croutons. Set aside.

Using a sharp knife, slice octopus on the diagonal into ¼-inch slices. Place octopus in a large salad bowl, add lemon juice and toss well. Add arugula, olives, and croutons and toss again. Drizzle with balsamic vinegar and the remaining ½ cup olive oil, then toss again. Season with salt and pepper.

TO SERVE Serve at room temperature.

Serves 10 to 12

Pacific Octopus, Dungeness Crab, and Sidestripe Shrimp Headcheese

ANGELO PROSPERI-PORTA, Cooper's Cove Guesthouse, Sooke, British Columbia

OCTOPUS British Columbia: *Best choice*; US: *Some concerns*

DUNGENESS CRAB *Best choice*

SHRIMP Trap-caught: *Best choice*; Trawled: *Some concerns*; Warm-water: *Avoid*

HEADCHEESE Wash octopus under cold running water. Place octopus in a large pot, cover with cold water, and bring to a simmer on medium-high heat. (Do not boil or the octopus will become tough.) Simmer for 20 to 30 minutes, periodically skimming off the foam that rises to the surface. Add onions, carrots, celery, garlic, bay leaves, parsley sprigs (or chervil, basil, or thyme), and lemon juice and simmer for 2 hours more, or until octopus is tender.

Line a 5-cup mould (such as a loaf pan) with plastic wrap or parchment paper. Rub the inside of the lined mould with olive oil. Cut a piece of cardboard to just fit the top of the mould.

Drain octopus using a colander. Discard poaching liquid and vegetables. While octopus is still warm, cut body and tentacles in ½ to 3¾-inch slices. Remove suction cups from the tentacles and discard. In a large bowl, combine octopus, shrimp meat, crabmeat, chopped parsley, and lemon zest. Season with salt and ground black pepper. Spoon the seafood mixture into the mould, being sure to press down firmly. Cover with a piece of parchment paper, fit the cardboard on top, then place 2 heavy cans or a brick on top of the cardboard. Refrigerate for several hours or preferably overnight.

continued overleaf...

HEADCHEESE

4 lbs Pacific octopus (body and tentacles)

1 onion, peeled and coarsely chopped

1 carrot, peeled and coarsely chopped

1 stalk celery, coarsely chopped

5 to 6 cloves garlic, peeled

3 bay leaves

Handful of Italian flat-leaf parsley sprigs or chervil, basil, or thyme, whole

Juice of 2 lemons

1 tsp olive oil

6 oz cooked sidestripe shrimp meat

10 oz Dungeness crabmeat, cooked and picked over for cartilage

¼ cup chopped fresh Italian flat-leaf parsley

Zest of 1 lemon, minced

BITTER GREENS SALAD

1 Tbsp dry sherry

2 Tbsp sherry vinegar

2 Tbsp honey

1 Tbsp Dijon mustard

1 Tbsp fresh lemon juice

1¼ cups extra-virgin olive oil

2 Tbsp finely diced
red bell peppers

1 Tbsp minced fresh
Italian flat-leaf parsley

1 small head radicchio,
in 8 wedges

1 cup curly endive leaves

BITTER GREENS SALAD Just before serving, whisk together sherry, sherry vinegar, honey, Dijon mustard, and lemon juice in a small bowl. Slowly add olive oil in a continuous stream, whisking until well emulsified. Whisk in red peppers and parsley.

Arrange radicchio and endive on a serving platter and drizzle with half of the dressing.

FINISH HEADCHEESE Remove headcheese from the refrigerator, lift off the weights, cardboard and parchment paper, and unmould onto a cutting board. If the mould does not release, dip it in a bowl of very hot water for 10 to 15 seconds. Dip a knife in hot water, then thinly slice the headcheese.

TO SERVE Arrange slices of headcheese on one side of the serving platter. Garnish with the salad. Drizzle the salad and the headcheese with the remaining dressing and serve.

Serves 8 as a first course

Giant Pacific Octopus with Tonnato Sauce

SUSUR LEE, Susur, Toronto

OCTOPUS British Columbia: *Best choice;* US: *Some concerns*

POACHED OCTOPUS In a large stockpot, combine onions, carrots, celery, fennel, bay leaves, parsley, thyme, peppercorns, fennel seeds, and water and bring to a boil on medium-high heat. Reduce the heat to low and simmer for 1 hour. Season with salt to taste.

Wash octopus under cold running water and add to the stock. Poach octopus until tender, about 2½ to 3½ hours. Drain the octopus and discard the vegetables.

Spread a 20 × 20-inch cheesecloth on a clean work surface. Separate octopus tentacles and lay them and any other pieces lengthwise, side by side, on the cheesecloth. Starting at one edge of the cheesecloth, tightly roll the material around the tentacles, encasing them in the cloth. Tie one end of the cheesecloth with an elastic band or a piece of butcher's twine. Starting at the tied end and working your way from one end of the tentacles to the other, gently squeeze the cheesecloth to push out all the fluid from the tentacles. Once all the fluid has been removed, tie closed the open end of the cheesecloth.

Transfer the wrapped octopus to a baking dish, cover with a small piece of cardboard, and weigh it down with a couple of heavy cans. Refrigerate the weighted dish for 12 hours or overnight.

continued overleaf...

POACHED OCTOPUS

4 onions, chopped

1 carrot, chopped

4 stalks celery

1 bulb fennel, sliced

3 bay leaves

6 sprigs Italian flat-leaf parsley, whole

3 sprigs thyme, whole

10 black peppercorns

1 Tbsp fennel seeds, roasted

16 cups water

6 to 8 lb octopus, fresh or defrosted if frozen

TONNATO SAUCE

¼ cup oil-packed
tuna, drained

2 Tbsp fresh lemon juice

1 Tbsp capers

4 Tbsp mayonnaise

1 tsp Worcestershire sauce

4 drops Tabasco sauce

2 tsp Dijon mustard

Pinch of granulated sugar

1 tsp white pepper

TONNATO SAUCE Using a blender, process all ingredients until smooth and well combined. Season with salt and refrigerate until ready to use. Will keep refrigerated in an airtight container for up to 2 weeks.

FINISH OCTOPUS Remove octopus from the refrigerator and lift off the weights and the cardboard. Unwrap the tentacles. If you prefer not to eat the suction cups, pull them off with your fingers. Using a sharp knife, slice the tentacles into thin rounds.

TO SERVE Arrange the slices of octopus on a serving platter and drizzle with the tonnato sauce.

Serves 8

Prairie Oyster Chowder

WADE SIROIS, Infuse Catering, Calgary

OYSTERS Farmed: *Best choice*; Wild: *Some concerns*

Heat a small stockpot on medium heat. Add bacon and fry until golden brown, 3 to 5 minutes. Drain all but ⅛ cup of the bacon fat. To the bacon, add onions and sauté until translucent, 1 to 2 minutes. Sprinkle onions with flour and stir for 1 minute.

Increase the heat to high and quickly add parsnips, carrots, and oysters. Stir gently for 1 minute, then add 1 cup of the fish stock (or water) and stir to deglaze the pan. Stir in the remaining fish stock (or water) and the wheat berries. Continue cooking on high heat until the chowder comes to a simmer, then reduce the heat to medium and simmer for 20 minutes.

To finish, add cream (or milk) and thyme and season with sea salt and freshly ground pepper.

TO SERVE Ladle the chowder into six warmed bowls. Enjoy immediately.

Serves 6

---

4 oz double-smoked bacon, finely diced

½ small onion, finely diced

⅛ cup unbleached white flour

½ cup peeled, shredded parsnips

½ cup peeled, shredded carrots

12 fresh farmed oysters, shucked and coarsely chopped, if desired

6 cups fish stock (page 21) or water

1 cup cooked wheat berries

½ cup whipping cream or half-and-half cream or skim milk

⅛ cup fresh thyme leaves or 2 tsp dried thyme

New Year's Eve Oyster Chowder

PATRICK MCMURRAY, Starfish Oyster Bed & Grill, Toronto

OYSTERS Farmed: *Best choice*; Wild: *Some concerns*

3 large potatoes,
peeled and diced

2 Tbsp + 1 tsp butter

6 stalks celery,
finely chopped

4 shallots, minced

12 large oysters, shucked

4 cups whole milk

1 cup whipping cream

2 slices extra-thick,
double-smoked bacon,
diced

24 small oysters, such as a
mix of small Hardy's and
Royal Malpeque, shucked

12 panko-crusted oysters
(page 134), for garnish

In a large saucepan on medium-high heat, boil potatoes in salted water until fork tender, about 5 minutes. Drain well, then set aside.

In another large saucepan set on low heat, melt the 2 Tbsp of butter. Add celery and shallots and sauté, without browning, until soft and shallots are translucent, about 10 minutes. Place the 12 large oysters on top of the celery mixture. Increase the heat to medium, cover, and cook (don't stir) for 5 minutes, or until the edges of the oysters ruffle like a tuxedo shirt. Using a slotted spoon, transfer oysters to a bowl and set aside. Reduce the heat to medium-low.

Add milk and cream to the celery mixture and heat through, being careful not to boil. Return the cooked oysters to the saucepan and add 1 cup of the cooked potatoes. Using a hand blender, purée the soup until smooth.

Line a plate with a paper bag. Heat a heavy frying pan on medium heat. Add bacon and fry until crisp, about 5 minutes. Using tongs, transfer bacon to the plate to drain.

Melt the 1 tsp of butter in a large saucepan on medium-low heat. Add the 24 small oysters, cover and cook until oysters ruffle and are just cooked through, 2 to 3 minutes. Pour in the soup and the remaining potatoes and heat through, being careful not to boil the chowder.

TO SERVE Divide the chowder among six warmed bowls, ensuring that the oysters are evenly distributed. Sprinkle each serving with bacon and garnish with two panko-crusted oysters.

Serves 6

Kaki Fry (Oyster Fry)

HIDEKAZU TOJO, Tojo's Restaurant, Vancouver

OYSTERS Farmed: *Best choice*; Wild: *Some concerns*

In a small saucepan, combine Worcestershire sauce with fish (or chicken) stock and ketchup on medium-high heat. Stir well.

In a small bowl, mix cornstarch and water until cornstarch dissolves. When the sauce is hot, stir in the cornstarch mixture and reduce the heat to medium. Whisk the sauce until thick, about 3 minutes, then stir in Tabasco and freshly ground black pepper to taste. Keep sauce warm on low heat, stirring occasionally.

Heat about 3 inches of canola oil in a deep-fryer or a deep heavy-bottomed pot on medium-high heat. Use a deep-frying thermometer to determine when it reaches 350°F. Be very careful with the hot oil.

Line a large plate with a paper bag and set aside. In a shallow dish, spread out flour. Place egg in another shallow dish and panko in a third.

Pat dry oysters with paper towels. Working with one oyster at a time, dredge in flour and shake off any excess. Then dip in egg and roll in panko to evenly coat. (Keep the coating light, as heavy batter overwhelms delicate seafood.) Deep-fry oysters in batches of 6 until golden brown, 3 to 5 minutes. Using a slotted spoon, transfer to the paper bag–lined plate to drain.

TO SERVE Arrange a mix of cabbage and tomato on four individual plates. Top with three oysters each and drizzle with some of the warm sauce.

Serves 4

1 cup Worcestershire sauce

½ cup fish stock (page 21) or chicken stock

2 Tbsp ketchup

1 Tbsp cornstarch

2 Tbsp water

3 drops of Tabasco sauce

6 to 8 cups canola oil

1 cup all-purpose flour

1 egg, lightly beaten

2 cups panko (Japanese bread crumbs)

12 Pacific beach oysters, shucked and unwashed

½ head cabbage, thinly sliced, for garnish

1 tomato, sliced, for garnish

Po'boy Oyster Sandwich and Shucker Paddy's Seaweed Caesar

PATRICK MCMURRAY, Starfish Oyster Bed & Grill, Toronto

OYSTERS Farmed: *Best choice*; Wild: *Some concerns*

OYSTER SANDWICH

1½ cups all-purpose flour

½ tsp salt

½ tsp pepper

3 eggs, beaten

2½ cups panko
(Japanese bread crumbs)

24 medium oysters, shucked

4 Tbsp olive oil

4 soft crusty buns, in half

4 Tbsp mayonnaise or
aioli or tartar sauce

8 lettuce leaves,
washed and dried

OYSTER SANDWICH Line a large plate with a paper bag and set aside. In a shallow dish, combine flour, salt, and pepper. Place eggs in another shallow dish. Fill a third shallow dish with panko. Working with one oyster at a time, dredge in flour and shake off any excess. Then dip in egg and roll in panko to evenly coat. (Keep the coating light, as heavy batter overwhelms delicate seafood.) Repeat until 6 of the oysters are coated.

Heat 2 Tbsp of the olive oil in a in a cast-iron frying pan on medium-high heat, making sure that the bottom of the pan is well coated. Carefully add coated oysters and fry until crisp and golden, 2 minutes per side. Using a slotted spoon, transfer oysters to the paper bag–lined plate to drain. Remove the pan from the heat.

Coat the remaining oysters in flour, egg, and panko. Wipe out the frying pan, then add the remaining olive oil and heat to medium-high. Pan-fry the remaining oysters and drain on the lined plate.

SEAWEED CAESAR Place dulse flakes on a small plate. Rub the outside rim of an 8 to 10-oz high-ball glass with a wedge of lime, then dip into dulse flakes.

Fill the glass with ice cubes. Add lime juice and Tabasco and Worcestershire sauces. Stir in vodka and a pinch of dulse flakes. Add horseradish, then Clamato. Garnish with a wedge of lime. Repeat as necessary!

TO SERVE Place the buns on a clean work surface. Spread the top half of each bun with 1 Tbsp of the mayonnaise (or aioli or tartar sauce). Line the bottom half of each bun with two lettuce leaves. Arrange 6 oysters on each bottom half, then assemble the sandwiches and serve with a cold Caesar on the side.

Serves 4

SEAWEED CAESAR

1 Tbsp flaked
dulse seaweed

½ lime, in 2 to 4 wedges

Ice cubes

Juice of ½ lime

2 dashes of Tabasco sauce

2 dashes of
Worcestershire sauce

1½ oz vodka, chilled

Pinch of freshly grated
horseradish or store-bought
horseradish, drained

6 oz Clamato juice

Oyster and Leek Stew

ROBERT CLARK, C Restaurant, Nu Restaurant, and Raincity Grill, Vancouver

OYSTERS Farmed: *Best choice*; Wild: *Some concerns*

2 Tbsp unsalted butter

¼ cup sliced shallots

1 cup diced potatoes

½ cup sliced leeks, white part only

2 cups whipping cream

Pinch of grated nutmeg

24 oysters

½ cup white wine

½ cup vermouth

Melt butter in a heavy-bottomed pot on medium heat. Add shallots, potatoes, and leeks, stirring often until translucent but not coloured, about 5 minutes. Pour in cream and season with salt, pepper, and nutmeg. Cover and cook until potatoes are tender, about 10 minutes.

While the potatoes are cooking, shuck oysters into a bowl. Discard the shells but reserve any liquor that escapes from the oysters.

Pour white wine and vermouth into a frying pan and bring to a boil on high heat. (Be careful if you are using a gas stove, as the alcohol may ignite if it comes in contact with a flame.) Carefully stir the oysters and their liquor into the simmering alcohol. After about 1 minute, remove from the heat. Using a slotted spoon, transfer the slightly poached oysters to a bowl.

Strain the oyster poaching liquid through a fine-mesh sieve into the leek and potato mixture, then bring to a simmer on high heat.

TO SERVE Divide the oysters among six warmed bowls. Spoon the hot soup over top.

Serves 6

Fanny Bay Oyster Pie

J.B. MacKINNON, author and 100-mile dieter, Vancouver

OYSTERS Farmed: *Best choice*; Wild: *Some concerns*

Fill a saucepan three-quarters full with water. Add potatoes and boil on medium-high heat until soft, 8 to 10 minutes. Drain, then mash until smooth. Set aside.

Working over a bowl, cut oysters into bite-size pieces with scissors. Reserve any oyster liquor in a small bowl. Lightly butter a 9-inch pie plate.

Preheat the oven to 350°F.

Melt the 2 Tbsp of butter in a medium frying pan on medium-low heat. Add celeriac and onions and sauté until celeriac is tender but not soft, about 5 minutes. Add oysters and cook just until the edges of the oysters start to curl, about 5 minutes. Remove from the heat and stir in eggs, parsley, salt, and hot pepper flakes. Lightly press the mixture into the prepared pie plate. Evenly drizzle oyster liquor over the top.

Spread mashed potatoes over the oyster mixture, completely covering it. Place the pie plate on a baking sheet and bake until the filling is hot, about 20 minutes. Brown the potato crust under the broiler, if you wish.

TO SERVE Cut the oyster pie into wedges and arrange on individual warmed plates. Serve with a seasonal salad and a dark beer.

Serves 4 to 6

4 Yukon Gold potatoes, peeled and cut in half

12 oysters, shucked

2 Tbsp butter

2 cups celeriac (celery root), chopped

1 large onion, diced

4 hard-cooked eggs, chopped

¼ cup chopped fresh Italian flat-leaf parsley

¼ tsp salt

¼ tsp hot red pepper flakes

Spot Prawn Gazpacho

ROBERT CLARK, C Restaurant, Nu Restaurant, and Raincity Grill, Vancouver

SPOT PRAWNS *Best choice*

2 large red bell peppers, coarsely chopped

⅓ English cucumber, peeled, seeded, and coarsely chopped

½ large red onion, coarsely chopped

2 cloves garlic, in half

2 cups canned plum tomatoes, puréed and strained

¾ cup fresh bread (optional)

2 Tbsp extra-virgin olive oil, or more

¼ cup red wine vinegar, or more

2 tsp Tabasco sauce

1 Tbsp granulated sugar

½ to 1 cup salt

2 lbs spot prawn tails

NOTE Adding the bread gives the soup a thicker texture. You may want more vinegar and oil if you use bread.

Place red peppers, cucumber, and onions in a glass or ceramic dish. Cover and refrigerate overnight.

In a food processor, combine the refrigerated vegetables, garlic, puréed tomatoes, bread, olive oil, red wine vinegar, Tabasco, and sugar. Season with salt and ground pepper and, if using bread, add 1 tsp more vinegar, or to taste. Purée until smooth, then strain the mixture through a fine-mesh sieve. Discard any remaining solids. Transfer to a bowl and refrigerate to allow the flavours to meld, about 30 minutes.

Fill a medium bowl with ice water. Bring a large pot of water to a boil on high heat. Add enough salt to make it taste like seawater, about ¼ cup salt per 4 cups water. Add prawns and boil for 30 seconds to 1 minute, or until prawns are just cooked. (Be very careful not to overcook the prawns, or they will be rubbery.) Using a slotted spoon, transfer the prawns to the bowl of ice water and allow them to cool. Peel the prawns and discard the shells.

TO SERVE Ladle the soup into four chilled bowls. Top each serving with cooked prawns.

Serves 4

Scallop Ceviche with Avocado and Cilantro

GORDON MACKIE, Far Niente Restaurant and Four, Toronto

SCALLOPS Farmed: *Best choice*; Wild, dive-caught: *Best choice*; Wild, dredged: *Avoid*

In a medium bowl, combine shallots, sugar, and salt. Allow to stand 5 minutes to release the shallot juices. Using a fork, mash together the shallot mixture.

Stir in lime juice and chili peppers, then add scallops and lime leaves. Allow to stand between 5 and 15 minutes. Pour off half the liquid and discard.

Stir in coconut milk and coarse salt, mixing gently to combine.

TO SERVE For an elegant presentation, divide the scallop mixture evenly among twelve Chinese soup spoons, then arrange them on a serving platter. Garnish the ceviche with avocado and sprinkle with cilantro. Serve immediately.

Serves 4 as a first course

- 2 small shallots, chopped
- 1 tsp granulated sugar
- 1 tsp salt
- Juice of 2 limes
- 1 tsp seeded and minced Anaheim chili pepper (or other mild green chili pepper)
- 1 lb pink or spiny scallops, shucked and chopped in small pieces
- 4 tsp kaffir lime leaves, finely chopped (available at specialty food stores and Asian food markets)
- 4 Tbsp coconut milk
- 1 tsp coarse salt
- 1 avocado, chopped, for garnish
- 4 tsp chopped fresh cilantro, for garnish

Maritime Scallops with Kumquat Chutney, Roasted Sunchokes, and Soy Bean Salad

ANTHONY WALSH, Canoe, Toronto

SCALLOPS Farmed: *Best choice*; Wild, dive-caught: *Best choice*; Wild, dredged: *Avoid*

KUMQUAT CHUTNEY
1 tsp coriander
seeds, crushed

½ tsp cardamom
seeds, crushed

½ tsp hot red pepper flakes

½ vanilla bean, cut in half

1 cup kumquats

⅓ cup granulated sugar

Juice of ½ lemon

¼ cup water

ROASTED SUNCHOKES
8 large sunchokes
(also known as Jerusalem
artichokes), washed
and cut in half

1 tsp chopped fresh
thyme leaves

1 clove garlic, sliced

2 Tbsp olive oil + 2 Tbsp
for drizzling

2 cups arugula, washed

2 cups dandelion greens
(or mustard greens or
Belgian endive leaves),
washed

2 celery hearts

KUMQUAT CHUTNEY Cut a piece of cheesecloth to 10 × 10 inches. Place coriander seeds, cardamom seeds, red pepper flakes, and vanilla bean in the middle of the cheesecloth. Bring the edges of the cheesecloth together and tie tightly with string.

Fill a saucepan three-quarters full with water. Bring to a boil on high heat, add kumquats and cook for 1 to 2 minutes. Transfer to a colander and run cold water over the kumquats to stop the cooking. Repeat two more times, then julienne the kumquats.

In a small saucepan on medium-high heat, combine sugar, lemon juice, and water until sugar dissolves. Add the spice sachet, cover, and simmer for 40 minutes. Remove and discard the spice sachet, then stir in kumquats. Transfer the chutney to a small bowl and refrigerate. Will keep refrigerated in an airtight container for up to 1 week.

ROASTED SUNCHOKES Preheat the oven to 350°F. In a bowl, toss sunchokes with thyme, garlic, and 2 Tbsp of the olive oil. Spread sunchokes on a baking sheet and roast until soft, about 30 minutes. Remove from the oven and set aside.

SOY BEAN SALAD On a clean work surface, lightly crush soy beans with a fork. Place them in a bowl and add shallots, chili peppers, lemon zest, lemon juice, and elderflower (or ice or white) wine. Whisk in olive oil, then season with salt and pepper.

SEARED SCALLOPS Preheat the oven to 475°F. Liberally season scallops with salt and pepper.

Heat vegetable oil in an ovenproof frying pan on medium-high heat. Add scallops and sear for 2 minutes per side. Remove from the heat and spoon 1 Tbsp of kumquat chutney over each scallop. Place in the oven and cook for 2 to 3 more minutes.

TO SERVE Arrange arugula, dandelion greens (or mustard greens or Belgian endive leaves), and celery hearts on four plates. Lightly drizzle with the remaining olive oil and season with salt and pepper. Place the sunchokes on the greens and top with two scallops per serving. Top with the soy bean salad.

Serves 4

SOY BEAN SALAD

1 cup shelled soy beans, cooked

2 shallots, minced

½ tsp minced Anaheim chili pepper (or other mild green chili pepper)

Zest of ½ lemon

1 Tbsp fresh lemon juice

1 tsp elderflower or ice wine or fruity white wine

1 Tbsp olive oil

SEARED SCALLOPS

8 large scallops

2 Tbsp vegetable oil

Maple-seared Scallops with Warm Mushroom Salad and Black Trumpet Vinaigrette

DAVID ROBERTSON, Chambar Restaurant, Vancouver

SCALLOPS Farmed: *Best choice*; Wild, dive-caught: *Best choice*; Wild, dredged: *Avoid*

BLACK TRUMPET VINAIGRETTE

1 package (½ oz) dried black trumpet mushrooms

⅓ cup sherry vinegar

1 small shallot, diced

1 clove garlic, minced

1 cup extra-virgin olive oil

2 tsp truffle oil

WARM MUSHROOM SALAD

2 tsp butter

4 shiitake mushrooms, stems removed and caps sliced

4 oyster mushrooms, sliced

1 tsp diced red onions

1 clove garlic, minced

½ cup white wine

MAPLE-SEARED SCALLOPS

2 Tbsp vegetable oil

¼ cup pure maple syrup

12 large scallops

¼ cup butter, cold and cubed

1 bunch watercress, washed and thick stems removed

1 small head frisée lettuce, washed and torn into small pieces

BLACK TRUMPET VINAIGRETTE Place mushrooms in a small bowl and add enough cold water to cover. Soak for 1 hour, then drain. Squeeze out and discard excess water from mushrooms. Finely chop mushrooms. Pour sherry vinegar into a bowl, then add mushrooms, shallots, and garlic. Whisk in the olive and truffle oils. Season with salt and cracked black pepper.

WARM MUSHROOM SALAD Melt butter in a small saucepan on medium heat. Add shiitake and oyster mushrooms, sprinkle with salt and cracked black pepper, and sauté for 2 minutes. Add onions and garlic and cook for 1 more minute. Pour in white wine and sauté, stirring often, until wine is reduced by half, 3 to 5 minutes. Set aside and cover to keep warm.

MAPLE-SEARED SCALLOPS Heat a frying pan on medium-high heat. When the pan is hot, add vegetable oil and coat well.

Pour maple syrup into a small bowl, then dip each scallop in the syrup to evenly coat. Add scallops to the pan in a single layer and sauté until golden, 1 minute per side. Season with salt and cracked black pepper, then add butter. Stir often until all of the butter has been absorbed.

TO SERVE Divide the scallops among four warmed bowls. Cover with the sautéed mushrooms, then garnish with watercress and frisée lettuce. Drizzle with the black trumpet vinaigrette.

Serves 4

Cider-glazed Spiny Scallops
with Warm Celery and Apple Slaw

KEVIN PRENDERGAST, Tundra Restaurant, Toronto

SCALLOPS Farmed: *Best choice*; Wild, dive-caught: *Best choice*;
Wild, dredged: *Avoid*

CIDER GLAZE Combine apple cider, honey, cinnamon, and thyme in a small saucepan on medium heat. Simmer until the liquid is reduced by half, about 15 minutes. Strain through a fine-mesh sieve, discarding any solids. Set aside. Will keep refrigerated in an airtight container for up to 1 week.

CELERY AND APPLE SLAW Melt butter in a frying pan on medium heat. When it foams, add apples, celery, celery leaves, and thyme. Season to taste with pinches of salt and white pepper. Stir until celery starts to soften, 2 to 3 minutes, then remove from the heat. Cover and set aside in a warm place, such as the back of the stove.

SCALLOPS Heat vegetable oil in a large frying pan on medium-high heat. Season scallops with salt, then sear until golden, 2 minutes per side. Pour 2 to 3 Tbsp of the cider glaze over the scallops, turning them until well coated. Remove from the heat.

TO SERVE Divide the scallops among four plates, then drizzle the warm glaze around them. Heap a few tablespoons of warm slaw on top of the scallops.

Serves 4

CIDER GLAZE
2 cups fresh apple cider

2 Tbsp wild honey

1 cinnamon stick

4 sprigs thyme, whole

CELERY AND APPLE SLAW
1 Tbsp butter

2 Granny Smith apples, peeled, cored, and cut in slivers

4 stalks celery, finely sliced

4 Tbsp celery leaves

1 Tbsp fresh thyme leaves

SCALLOPS
2 Tbsp vegetable oil

1 lb spiny scallops

Scallops with Collard Greens and Pernod Sabayon

ROLAND AND KATHLEEN GLAUSER, Charlotte Lane Restaurant, Shelburne, Nova Scotia

SCALLOPS Farmed: *Best choice*; Wild, dive-caught: *Best choice*; Wild, dredged: *Avoid*

SCALLOPS WITH COLLARD GREENS

2 tsp butter

2 tsp olive oil

2 cups collard greens, washed and chopped

1 small shallot, chopped

1 large clove garlic, minced

1 tsp chopped fresh ginger

2 Tbsp sake (Japanese rice wine)

2 Tbsp tamari or soy sauce

1 tsp balsamic vinegar

16 to 20 large sea scallops (about 1 lb)

SCALLOPS WITH COLLARD GREENS Preheat the oven to 400°F.

Place butter and olive oil in a large frying pan on medium heat. When the butter foams, add collard greens, shallots, garlic, and ginger and sauté for 2 minutes. Add sake, tamari (or soy sauce), and balsamic vinegar. Bring to a boil and cook until the liquid is reduced by half, about 7 minutes. Season with salt and pepper.

Place 4 large scallop shells or 4 small ramekins on a baking sheet. Divide scallops among the shells (or ramekins). (If you have neither of these, arrange scallops in a large shallow ovenproof dish.) Spoon the collard green mixture evenly over the scallops. Bake in the centre of the oven for 10 to 12 minutes, until scallops are firmer and more opaque. Remove from the heat and set aside on the tray. While the scallops are baking, make the sabayon.

PERNOD SABAYON In the top of a double boiler or in a small stainless steel bowl, combine eggs, white wine, Pernod, lemon juice, Worcestershire sauce, and pinches of salt and pepper.

In the bottom of the double boiler, or a pot large enough to hold the stainless steel bowl, bring about an inch of water to a simmer on medium heat. Place the egg mixture over the hot water and, using a whisk, beat vigorously until the sauce is fluffy and thick, about 2 minutes. Remove from the heat.

FINISH SCALLOPS Preheat the broiler. Spoon the sauce over the scallops, then broil until the sauce is golden, about 5 minutes.

TO SERVE Place a scallop shell or a ramekin on each warmed plate (or dish up four to five scallops per person from the ovenproof dish). Serve immediately.

Serves 4

PERNOD SABAYON
2 large eggs
2 Tbsp white wine
2 Tbsp Pernod
½ tsp fresh lemon juice
½ tsp Worcestershire sauce

Pan-seared Scallops with Leek and Tarragon Sauce

TRISH MAGWOOD, Dish Cooking Studio, Toronto

SCALLOPS Farmed: *Best choice*; Wild, dive-caught: *Best choice*; Wild, dredged: *Avoidd*

PAN-SEARED SCALLOPS

18 medium sea scallops (10/20 size)

2 to 4 Tbsp canola oil or grapeseed oil

1 head frisée lettuce, washed, dried, and torn into pieces

2 tsp olive oil

LEEK AND TARRAGON SAUCE

1 Tbsp butter

1 tsp olive oil

2 shallots, sliced

2 leeks, white and light green parts only, washed and sliced

3 cloves garlic, minced

1/2 cup white wine

1/2 cup whipping cream

1/2 bunch fresh tarragon, finely chopped

PAN-SEARED SCALLOPS Pat scallops dry with a clean tea towel. Season scallops on both sides with salt and freshly cracked pepper. Heat a large, heavy frying pan on high heat. Pour in just enough canola (or grapeseed) oil to coat the bottom of the pan.

Add scallops and sear for 1 to 2 minutes per side, or until golden. (If the pan is not large enough to hold all the scallops at once, you may need to sear them in batches). Transfer scallops to a plate.

LEEK AND TARRAGON SAUCE Return the frying pan to high heat and add butter and olive oil. Stir in shallots and leeks and sauté until fragrant, about 5 minutes. Add garlic and sauté for another 3 minutes.

Deglaze the pan with white wine and reduce to 1/4 cup, 2 to 3 minutes. Add cream and reduce by about half, or until the sauce coats the back of a spoon, about 5 minutes. Stir in tarragon and season with salt and pepper.

TO SERVE In a small bowl, lightly toss frisée lettuce with olive oil and a pinch of salt. Arrange the greens in the centre of six plates and top each serving with three scallops. Drizzle with the leek and tarragon sauce.

Serves 6

Winter Sea Urchin Salad

DAVID FEYS (former chef) AND SINCLAIR PHILIP,
Sooke Harbour House, Sooke, British Columbia

SEA URCHIN *Best choice*

NOTE Sea urchin roe should be orange and have the scent of tropical fruit. A granular yellow roe will smell and taste of iodine. Do not substitute roe preserved in alum or frozen, as it quickly loses its flavour. Sea urchin is best during the winter months.

In a small saucepan, combine half the pear cider with the white wine and shallots. Bring to a boil on medium-high heat and reduce to a third. Remove from the heat and allow to cool.

Turn the sea urchin so that the mouth is flat on a cutting surface. Using a large knife, cut directly down the centre of the urchin. Open the urchin, then remove the orange strips with your fingers. Using a small spoon, discard any black substances or seaweed. Rinse the orange roe in a colander or in your hands under cold running water.

Place the roe in a blender or food processor. Add the cider reduction and 1 Tbsp of the sunflower oil. Blend until completely smooth.

Pour the puréed roe mixture into a small bowl and fold in the whipped cream. Stir in the fennel and 2 Tbsp of the pear cider (save leftover cider for another use). Taste the dressing, and add a drop of vinegar, if desired. Refrigerate no longer than a few hours since sea urchin loses its fruity, mango-like flavour quite quickly.

TO SERVE Heap salad greens in the centre of six plates. Ladle the urchin dressing around the greens, then drizzle with the remaining sunflower oil.

Serves 6

1 bottle (12 oz) sparkling pear cider

¼ cup Riesling or other dry white wine

1 shallot, minced

1 fresh sea urchin (preferably green) or 2 oz sea urchin roe

3 Tbsp sunflower oil

½ cup whipping cream, whipped

1 Tbsp finely chopped fresh fennel tops

⅛ tsp white wine vinegar (optional)

12 cups fresh salad greens (include a mix of herbs such as French sorrel, mint, or ox-eye daisy, as available)

Shrimp Coconut Soup

GORDON MACKIE, Far Niente Restaurant and Four, Toronto

SIDESTRIPE SHRIMP Trap-caught: *Best choice*;
Trawled: *Some concerns*; Warm-water: *Avoid*

1 Tbsp vegetable oil

1 Tbsp chopped fresh garlic

2 Tbsp grated fresh ginger

1 stem lemon grass,
smashed (available
at Asian food markets)

4 Tbsp Thai
yellow curry paste

3 cans (each 14 oz)
coconut milk

2 cups chicken stock

6 Tbsp brown sugar

Juice of 1 lime

3 Tbsp Thai fish sauce

1 lb medium sidestripe
shrimp, peeled and
deveined, cut in half

¾ cup bean
sprouts, for garnish

4 Tbsp cilantro
leaves, for garnish

1 lime, in 4 wedges,
for garnish

Place vegetable oil, garlic, ginger, and lemon grass in a large stockpot and gently warm on medium-low heat for 2 to 3 minutes, to release the aromas. Stir in curry paste, then add coconut milk and chicken stock. Increase the heat to medium and bring the mixture to a simmer. Add sugar, lime juice, and fish sauce, stirring continuously.

Using a slotted spoon, remove and discard lemon grass. Add shrimp and cook for about 2 minutes, until the shrimp are opaque and just cooked through. Using the slotted spoon, remove shrimp and divide evenly among 4 bowls.

TO SERVE Ladle broth over the shrimp. Garnish each serving with bean sprouts, cilantro leaves, and a wedge of lime.

Serves 4

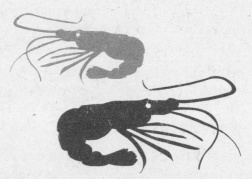

Shrimp, Shiitake, and Cucumber Salad with Basil–Coconut Milk Dressing

MARC DE CANCK, Restaurant La Chronique, Montreal

SHRIMP Trap-caught: *Best choice*; Trawled: *Some concerns*; Warm-water: *Avoid*

Fill a medium bowl with ice water and set aside. Fill a small saucepan three-quarters full with water and bring to a boil on high heat. Using a sharp knife, cut an X in the bases of the tomatoes, then submerge them in the boiling water for 5 seconds. Using a slotted spoon, transfer tomatoes to the bowl of ice water until cool enough to handle. Peel and discard the skins. Cut tomatoes in half, scoop out and discard the seeds, then chop the flesh into a small dice. Set aside.

In a large frying pan, heat olive oil on high heat. Add shrimp and sauté for 30 seconds per side. Season with celery salt and black pepper, then transfer the shrimp to a large bowl. Reduce the heat to medium.

Place mushrooms in the frying pan and sauté for 1 minute. Stir in cucumber, tomatoes, mirin, and coconut milk and cook for about 3 minutes, or until warmed through. Remove from the heat and pour over the shrimp. Gently stir in 12 of the basil leaves.

TO SERVE Divide the fried noodles between two plates, then top each serving with six shrimp and half the dressing. Garnish with the reserved basil leaves. Serve immediately.

Serves 2

2 tomatoes

4 Tbsp olive oil

12 large shrimp, peeled and deveined

1 tsp celery salt

½ tsp black pepper

10 shiitake mushrooms, stemmed and caps minced

1 English cucumber, peeled and julienned

4 Tbsp mirin (Japanese rice wine)

½ cup unsweetened coconut milk

16 fresh Thai basil leaves, washed and dried

2 small handfuls fried vermicelli noodles

Charred Sidestripe Shrimp Salad
with Truffle Orange Dressing

KEVIN PRENDERGAST, Tundra Restaurant, Toronto

SHRIMP Trap-caught: *Best choice*; Trawled: *Some concerns*;
Warm-water: *Avoid*

TRUFFLE ORANGE DRESSING

1 large shallot, minced

1½ Tbsp champagne
vinegar or white
wine vinegar

½ cup freshly
squeezed orange juice

½ cup vegetable oil

2 Tbsp white truffle oil

CHARRED SIDESTRIPE
SHRIMP SALAD

1 lb sidestripe
shrimp, peeled

1 Tbsp smoked paprika

1 Tbsp olive oil

2 avocados, diced

2 cups corn kernels, cooked

2 Tbsp chopped
fresh Italian flat-leaf
parsley, for garnish

TRUFFLE ORANGE DRESSING In a bowl, combine shallots with champagne vinegar (or white wine vinegar). Season with pinches of salt and white pepper and allow to stand at room temperature for 5 minutes. Whisk in orange juice, vegetable oil, and truffle oil. Set aside. Will keep refrigerated in an airtight container for up to 4 days.

CHARRED SIDESTRIPE SHRIMP SALAD Place shrimp in a large bowl. Add paprika and toss to coat evenly. Heat olive oil in a large frying pan on medium-high heat. Add shrimp and stir-fry until shrimp are cooked through and slightly charred, 3 to 4 minutes. Remove from the heat and allow to cool to room temperature.

Combine avocado and corn in a large bowl, then add shrimp. Drizzle with 2 Tbsp of the dressing and toss well. Season to taste with salt and pepper. If necessary, add more dressing to lightly coat the salad and toss again.

TO SERVE Spoon the salad evenly among four plates and sprinkle each serving with parsley.

Serves 4

Chedabucto Bay Shrimp and Prosciutto Biscuits

CRAIG FLINN, Chives Canadian Bistro, Halifax

SHRIMP Trap-caught: *Best choice*; Trawled: *Some concerns*; Warm-water: *Avoid*

BISCUITS Preheat the oven to 425°F. Position the rack in the centre of the oven. In a bowl, stir together flour, sugar, baking powder, and sea salt. Using 2 knives or a pastry blender, cut butter into the flour mixture until it resembles coarse meal.

In another bowl, whisk egg with the 1¼ cups buttermilk. Pour over the flour mixture and gently stir until a dough forms. Don't overmix, or the biscuits will be tough.

On a clean work surface, roll out the dough until it is 1 inch thick. Using a 3-inch round cutter or a glass rim, cut the dough into 8 to 10 circles. Place the biscuits on a baking sheet and brush the tops with buttermilk. Bake until golden, about 12 minutes. Remove from the oven and allow to cool.

PROSCIUTTO AND SHRIMP Line a plate with a paper bag. Heat the 3 Tbsp olive oil in a frying pan on medium-high heat. Working in batches (don't crowd the pan), fry prosciutto until crispy, 3 to 5 minutes. Transfer to the paper bag–lined plate to drain. Reserve the pan.

With a sharp knife, slice biscuits in half horizontally. Brush the cut sides of the biscuits with a little olive oil. Place the reserved frying pan on medium heat and fry the biscuits, cut side down, until crisp and golden, 3 to 5 minutes. Work in batches, if necessary. Set fried biscuits aside and keep warm.

continued overleaf…

BISCUITS

- 4 cups all-purpose flour
- 4 tsp granulated sugar
- 4 tsp baking powder
- 1 tsp sea salt
- 1 cup butter
- 1 egg
- 1¼ cups buttermilk
  + 2 Tbsp for brushing

PROSCIUTTO AND SHRIMP

3 Tbsp olive oil
+ 2 Tbsp for brushing

8 to 10 slices prosciutto

3 Tbsp butter

6 cloves garlic, minced

1 shallot, minced

1½ lbs shrimp or prawns,
peeled and deveined

¼ cup brandy

¼ cup chicken stock
or vegetable stock

1 cup whipping cream

¼ cup freshly grated
Parmesan cheese
+ 2 Tbsp for garnish

3 Tbsp chopped fresh
Italian flat-leaf parsley

10 sprigs fresh
Italian flat-leaf
parsley, for garnish

Melt butter in a separate large frying pan on medium heat. Add garlic and shallots and sauté for 2 minutes. Increase the heat to medium-high, add shrimp, and cook for 2 minutes. Remove the pan from the heat.

Measure brandy into a measuring cup. (Pouring directly from the bottle into a hot pan can cause the vapours to lead back into the bottle and build enough pressure for the bottle to explode.) Pour brandy into the pan of shrimp and return it to the heat. Stand away from the stove and use a barbecue lighter or a long fireplace match to light the fumes of the alcohol at the edge of the pan. (Be careful to keep your hair and any loose clothing away from the pan, as the flames will rush up.) Allow the flames to burn for 2 minutes. If necessary, cover with a lid to put out the flames.

Stir in chicken (or vegetable) stock and cream, then boil until the sauce is reduced by half, about 3 minutes. (The sauce should be light but not too thick.) Remove from the heat and stir in the ¼ cup of Parmesan cheese and the chopped parsley. Season with salt and freshly ground black pepper.

TO SERVE Place the bottom halves of the biscuits on individual plates. Lay a piece of crisped prosciutto on each one and top with spoonfuls of shrimp. Lean the top halves of the biscuits against the shrimp. Garnish each serving with a sprig of parsley and some grated Parmesan cheese.

Serves 8 to 10

Sidestripe Shrimp Gyoza

TIM CUFF, British Columbia

SHRIMP Trap-caught: *Best choice;*
Trawled: *Some concerns;* Warm-water: *Avoid*

Melt butter in a large, heavy-bottomed sauce-pan on medium heat. Add shallots, garlic, ginger, lemon grass, and sesame oil and sauté, stirring often, for 2 minutes.

In a bowl, toss shrimp with chives, then add to the pan. Sauté, stirring often, until shrimp are just cooked through, about 2 minutes. Stir in lime juice, salt, and pepper. Transfer the shrimp mix-ture to a bowl and refrigerate until cool.

Place 3 gyoza wrappers on a clean, dry work surface (keep the remaining wrappers covered with a damp towel). Dollop 1 to 2 tsp of the shrimp mixture in the centre of each wrapper. (Do not overfill the wrappers or you will not be able to close them.) There should be a ¾-inch border without filling around the edge of each wrapper. Dip your finger or a pastry brush in water and moisten the edges of the wrappers. One at a time, fold the top half of each wrapper over the bottom half to make a half-moon shape, squeezing the filling slightly with your fingers so it is completely enclosed.

continued overleaf…

2 Tbsp butter

1 shallot, diced

1 clove garlic, minced

½ tsp grated fresh ginger

½ tsp finely grated lemon grass (available at Asian food markets)

½ tsp sesame oil

32 sidestripe shrimp, peeled and deveined, cut in ⅓-inch pieces

3 chives, sliced

Juice of ½ lime

¼ tsp salt

¼ tsp pepper

1 lb gyoza wrappers (3-inch diameter)

2 Tbsp vegetable oil

½ cup dashi (Japanese soup stock) or chicken stock, hot

Press the edges of the wrapper together tightly, then, beginning at one end, pinch the edges between your fingers, creating 5 or 6 folds, or pleats. Fill and fold the remaining wrappers until all the filling is used. You should have about 24 filled gyoza.

Heat vegetable oil in a frying pan on medium heat. Add 6 to 8 gyoza and pan-fry on one side until golden, about 2 minutes. Using tongs, turn gyoza over, add a quarter of the dashi (or chicken stock) and cover. Steam the gyoza for 2 minutes, then transfer them to a warm platter using a slotted spoon. Wipe out the pan, and repeat with the remaining gyoza.

TO SERVE Serve warm, about four gyoza per person, with soy sauce for dipping.

Serves 6 as a first course

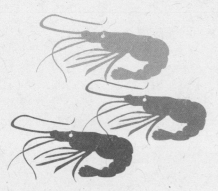

Sautéed Calamari and Spicy Chorizo Salad

ROMEO OLORESISIMO, A Kettle of Fish, Vancouver

Second-place winner, SeaChoice Culinary Competition

SQUID Pacific: *Best choice*; Atlantic: *Some concerns*

Heat vegetable oil in a large frying pan on medium heat. Add shallots, garlic, and chorizo and sauté for 5 minutes. Add squid and sauté until cooked through, 4 to 5 minutes. Stir in butter and tomatoes, then season with salt and pepper. Remove the pan from the heat and fold in spinach leaves. Allow the spinach to wilt slightly.

TO SERVE Mound the squid and sausage in equal portions on warmed plates and top with the wilted spinach. Serve immediately.

Serves 2

1 Tbsp vegetable oil

1 shallot, sliced

1 clove garlic, minced

1 chorizo sausage, cooked and cut in ¼-inch rounds

12 oz squid, tubes and tentacles, cleaned and cut in 1-inch pieces

1 Tbsp butter

10 grape tomatoes or cherry tomatoes, in half

4 oz spinach leaves

Shredded Grilled Calamari with Basil Purée and Preserved Lemon

DAVID FERGUSON, Restaurant Le Jolifou, Montreal

SQUID Pacific: *Best choice*; Atlantic: *Some concerns*

PRESERVED LEMONS
4 lemons

1 cup salt

GRILLED SQUID
1 bunch basil, leaves only

¼ cup grapeseed oil

1 lb squid, tubes and tentacles only, cleaned

1 preserved lemon or 1 Tbsp lemon zest

¼ French shallot, thinly sliced

1 Tbsp champagne vinegar or good-quality white wine vinegar

PRESERVED LEMONS Sterilize a 4-cup wide-mouth glass jar with a tight-fitting lid by submerging it in boiling water for 1 to 2 minutes. Remove from the water and allow to cool and air dry in a dish rack at room temperature.

Using a sharp knife and starting at the pointed end of the fruit, slice each lemon lengthwise in 4 sections, cutting three-quarters of the way through the fruit but leaving the sections joined at the base. Open the lemons like flowers and pack them inside and out with salt.

Gently squeeze the juice from the lemons into the glass jar. Then place the lemons in the jar, pushing them down so they are completely covered with lemon juice and salt. Tightly seal the jar and allow the lemons to marinate at room temperature. After 3 days, stir lemons, juice, and salt and pack down tightly. Tightly seal the jar and allow the lemons to marinate for 3 weeks. Remove lemons from the salt mixture and transfer to an airtight container. Will keep for up to 1 month.

GRILLED SQUID Fill a bowl with ice water. Bring a large pot of water to a boil on high heat. Reserving 4 to 6 leaves for garnish, immerse the basil in the boiling water. Blanch for about 5 seconds, then use a slotted spoon to transfer the leaves immediately to the bowl of ice water. Chill them for another 5 seconds. Remove the basil and dry the leaves very well. Place basil in a blender, just cover with grapeseed oil, and blend until smooth. Set aside.

Preheat a grill or a barbecue to medium-high heat. Rinse squid under cold running water and pat dry. Lightly score each squid in 3 places, about 1½ inches apart. In a bowl, toss squid with 1 Tbsp of grapeseed oil and season with salt and pepper. Grill squid, turning it occasionally, until lightly coloured, about 10 minutes. Transfer squid to a cutting board.

Using a sharp knife, cut tubes widthwise into 3 sections. (This will give you 3 rings per tube.) Cut open each ring to create a band. Finely slice crosswise through each band to make strips 1½ inches wide. Place these strips in a bowl.

Remove a preserved lemon from the salt mixture and rinse off any excess salt. Finely dice the skin of the preserved lemon (you should have at least 1 Tbsp) and add it to the squid (or use fresh lemon zest). Stir in 3 Tbsp of the basil purée and the shallots. Add champagne vinegar (or white wine vinegar) and salt to taste, then toss gently.

TO SERVE Arrange the calamari on a platter and garnish with whole basil leaves.

Serves 4 to 6 as a first course

Cornmeal-crusted Calamari with Chili Aioli

STEVE LEMIEUX, Le Bouchon de Liège, Montreal

SQUID Pacific: *Best choice;* Atlantic: *Some concerns*

MARINADE

1 cup milk

1 tsp ground coriander

1 tsp ground cumin

1 tsp garlic powder

1 tsp onion powder

1 tsp white pepper

1 tsp tandoori spice (available at Indian food stores) or Cajun spice mix

1 tsp celery salt

½ tsp sambal oelek or hot chili sauce

CORNMEAL-CRUSTED CALAMARI

3½ lbs squid, cleaned, tubes sliced in 1/2-inch pieces, tentacles cut in half

1 cup cornmeal

1 cup all-purpose flour

1 tsp ground coriander

1 tsp ground cumin

1 tsp garlic powder

1 tsp onion powder

1 tsp white pepper

1 tsp tandoori spice or Cajun spice mix

1 tsp celery salt

½ cup canola oil, or more

MARINADE In a bowl, combine milk, coriander, cumin, garlic powder, onion powder, white pepper, tandoori spice (or Cajun spice mix), celery salt, and sambal oelek (or chili sauce). Will keep refrigerated in an airtight container for up to 24 hours.

CORNMEAL-CRUSTED CALAMARI Place the marinade in a dish, add squid, and cover with a lid. Marinate in the refrigerator for at least 12 hours. Drain squid, discarding the marinade. Refrigerate the squid until needed, or for up to 4 days in an airtight container.

Line a plate with a clean tea towel. In a shallow dish, combine cornmeal, flour, coriander, cumin, garlic powder, onion powder, white pepper, tandoori spice (or Cajun spice mix), and celery salt. Dredge the squid in the cornmeal mixture, shaking off any excess.

In a large, straight-sided frying pan, heat canola oil on medium-high heat until it sizzles when a drop of water is added. Carefully add squid and fry until golden brown, turning once, about 4 minutes in total. (If the pan is not large enough to hold all the squid at once, you may want to sear it in batches. Add more oil as needed.) Transfer the calamari to the towel-lined plate to drain.

CHILI AIOLI Using a food processor or an electric mixer, blend mayonnaise, chili peppers, garlic, and lemon juice until smooth. Season with salt and white pepper. Refrigerate in an airtight container until ready to serve. Will keep refrigerated for up to 2 weeks.

TO SERVE Place calamari on a platter and serve warm with a bowl of chili aioli for dipping.

Serves 4 as a first course

CHILI AIOLI

1 cup mayonnaise

2 small fresh hot red chili peppers, seeded and finely chopped

3 large cloves garlic, minced

2 Tbsp fresh lemon juice

Making Sustainable Choices

Sustainable fisheries have historically been run on the principle of "sustainable yield," where the target fish or shellfish is replaced at a rate equal to what is removed. Today, however, growing concerns surrounding climate change and the environment have also made such issues as the amount of fossil fuel used to harvest fish and shellfish an important factor in determining sustainability. Because the complexities of both the ecological system (for example, the oceans) and the human system (for example, governments and communities) can make assessing the priorities extremely difficult, the David Suzuki Foundation outlines ten principles to guide our efforts in promoting sustainable fisheries:

1. Manage the entire marine ecosystem, rather than individual stocks.

2. Adopt a precautionary approach to fisheries management.

3. Ensure that all relevant parties have a meaningful say in fisheries management.

4. Decrease fishing fleet capacity and plan for stock fluctuations.

5. Protect critical ecological and species diversity.

6. Protect critical ocean habitat.

7. Create marine reserves to protect representative marine habitats.

8. Manage and minimize bycatch and discards in commercial fisheries.

9. Ensure that aquaculture operates under sustainable standards.

10. Invest in monitoring, enforcement, and data acquisition.

With several marine species at risk of disappearing, it's important we manage our fisheries carefully, choose our seafood wisely, and fish sustainably.

Fish is now the world's most-traded animal commodity, according to a recently published article in the *New York Times*: about one hundred million tons of wild and farmed fish are sold on the global market each year. Some of this catch has been harvested illegally or under very poor management conditions. By learning more about the fish you buy, you can help to ensure that it is harvested properly and legally. Simply asking your supplier to identify the species, and to provide information about where it was caught and how, is a significant step toward creating a chain of custody.

ASSESSING FISHING METHODS

Fishing methods vary widely in the effect they have on our environment and on the health of the marine ecosystem.

The best-choice methods include *hook-and-line fishing*, in which fishers use a pole hung with one to several baited hooks. They jerk the line to mimic the motion of smaller fish, which is known as "jigging." Unwanted catch can be released quickly. *Trolling* is another good choice, in which hook-and-line gear is towed behind the boat. Both hook-and-line fishing and trolling are used in coastal waters and inland. Fish caught by *harpoon* are a good choice, as are shellfish *harvested by divers*. Fishing with *traps and pots* is a sustainable method used to catch fish and harvest shellfish, as there is little bycatch and much of it can be released alive. Also, environmental damage is very minimal with these methods.

Methods with some concerns include *long-lining*, which uses single fishing lines hung with hundreds (or even thousands) of baited hooks and laid down by boat. Fishers leave these lines in the water for several hours or overnight and then return to haul them in. *Pelagic long-lining* simply means "out in the open water," whether the ocean or a lake, away from the shoreline and bottom. In *demersal long-lining*, hooks are floated just off the bottom to catch fish such as cod or halibut. Long-line hooks can catch many unwanted species, including endangered sea turtles. By using special circular hooks and setting their lines deeper, long-liners can reduce the amount of bycatch. Long-lining can also be a risk for sea birds: when the lines are set into the water, the birds are attracted to the bait and sometimes get caught on the hooks and drown.

Seining uses a large wall of nets held vertical with weights on the bottom and floats on the top to enclose a school of fish, such as sardines, or a group that has gathered to spawn, such as squid. A purse seine is a net with rings along the bottom and a rope run through them and is often used to catch fish that gather close to the surface. When the rope is pulled, the bottom of the net closes, trapping the fish inside. Fishers haul the nets aboard a boat or simply scoop up the fish. Purse seining can result in large amounts of bycatch.

Like seining, *gillnetting* uses large nets that hang in the water, positioned by floats and weights. Gillnets are used on the ocean as well as on lakes and rivers. Whereas seining contains fish within closed nets, gillnetting traps fish as they swim into the mesh of the nets. The size of the mesh determines which species of fish are caught, since fish that are too big to squeeze forward through the mesh also cannot back out, as their gills tend to get caught up in the net. Significant amounts of bycatch, including marine mammals and turtles, can be trapped in gillnets. Gillnets anchored to the sea floor can also damage habitat when they are hauled in, as they often get tangled on rocks or coral.

Of more concern is *trawling,* which involves dragging a cone-shaped net behind a boat to scoop up fish. Floats are used to keep the upper edge of the net opening higher than the weighted bottom edge, thereby creating a net with a mouth at one end and a closed tail at the other. Weighted nets are used to harvest shrimp and flounder, which are stirred up from the bottom. Trawl nets can catch significant amounts of bycatch, depending on how the nets are set, and weighted nets can damage the ocean floor.

Dredging involves dragging a metal frame with a net bag attached along the ocean floor, picking up the bottom-dwelling clams, oysters, scallops, and other shellfish, along with bycatch. Dredging causes significant habitat destruction; however, if the area to be dredged is small (for example, in a mussel farm), the impact of dredging may be considered of moderate concern.

ASSESSING AQUACULTURE

Humans have been farming fish for centuries. As the demand for fish and shellfish rises, we will need to expand our aquaculture resources; in many cases, relying exclusively on wild stocks is not a viable option. However, those wild stocks remain a precious resource, as is the natural aquatic environment, and we need to ensure that our farming practices don't harm wild species or the underwater world in which they live.

Canada produces some of the best fish and shellfish in the world. Aquaculture is big business here, accounting for more than 20 per cent of our seafood harvest. In every Canadian province and in the Yukon Territory, fish are farmed successfully, although the species and farming methods vary. In some cases, eating a farmed fish is a more sustainable choice than eating a wild one.

Four species of saltwater fish are farmed in Canada: Atlantic salmon, chinook salmon, coho salmon, and steelhead. Atlantic salmon is the main cultivated saltwater fish. Freshwater fish that are farmed in Canada include Arctic char, tilapia, brook trout, and rainbow trout. Rainbow trout is the main domestically raised freshwater fish. Scientists are also experimenting with rearing striped bass, Atlantic cod, haddock, halibut, sablefish, and wolffish. Other species, such as tuna, are farmed in different parts of the world.

Shellfish is also farmed in Canada. Prince Edward Island is the largest shellfish producer, followed by British Columbia, Nova Scotia, New Brunswick, Newfoundland and Labrador, and Quebec. Six species of bivalve shellfish are currently being raised in Canada: geoduck clam, Manila clam, blue mussel, American oyster, Pacific oyster, and scallop. Scientists are also experimenting with farming northern abalone, bar clam, quahaug (hard-shell clam), soft-shell clam, and sea urchin.

There are several different types of fish farms in common use in Canada, including open-net, closed-system, raceways, and beach aquaculture.

Open-net farming involves placing pens or cages made of nets in open water. These types of farms are located near to shore on the coast, farther out in the open ocean, and in lakes. Since the water circulates freely in and around these net cages, fish and shellfish are often cultivated in hatcheries (where the temperature and other conditions necessary for breeding can more easily be controlled) and then raised to maturity in these farms; sometimes, wild fish are caught and then held in open-net farms, where they are fed and fattened for market. Salmon are typically farmed using this method.

Open-net farming operations have been the subject of intense debate, particularly in British Columbia, where the salmon farms of the Broughton Archipelago threaten the wild pink salmon population. On a small scale, open-net farming may not cause serious problems, but some operations are large and intensive, raising thousands of fish. When the scale increases, so do the problems. Waste from the fish drops out of the pens and cages directly into the water and can be a significant cause of habitat pollution. Diseases and parasites, such as sea lice, can be spread to wild fish living or swimming near the open-net farms, and measures taken to treat these problems, such as using antibiotics, can also affect natural waters. Farmed fish can escape and threaten wild stocks by interbreeding with them and competing for natural resources such as food. There is now a moratorium on new fish farms on the north coast of British Columbia, as researchers try to resolve these problems.

Closed-system farming, or raising fish in closed containers made of aluminum, concrete, or fibreglass, which are located on land and filled with recirculating water, may be more sustainable than using conventional open nets. Providing the effluent is treated before it is discharged, these fish farms do not destroy local habitat and they eliminate the risk of farmed fish escaping and intermingling with wild stocks. Closed systems also include ponds, where freshwater fish such as tilapia and trout are cultivated. Ponds can also be used to raise saltwater species such as shrimp.

Some companies are experimenting with farming salmon in closed containers. While raising salmon this way minimizes some of the environmental damage associated with fish farming, it requires significant amounts of energy to keep the water recirculating and the systems running constantly. Farm-raised carnivorous fish, such as salmon, consume huge amounts of feed, and this feed is made from other species of fish, which contributes to the overall depletion of the ocean.

Raceways are artificial channels through which water is continuously pumped. They are used to raise freshwater fish, such as trout, in inland fish farms. The water can be treated to reduce the negative effects of the effluent before the water is returned to a natural waterway. However, if the raceway is located near a natural waterway, there is the possibility of the farmed stock escaping and threatening wild stocks.

Beach aquaculture refers to farming shellfish at the beach, on or near the sea floor, or in deep water. Bottom aquaculture takes place in the intertidal zone and is used to farm shellfish such as clams or oysters. Near-bottom aquaculture is also used in the intertidal zone, but the shellfish, such as scallops or mussels, are raised off the sea floor, on stakes, on racks, or in mesh bags. Shellfish are also raised in the deep water, suspended on long lines or in trays or mesh bags. Because these shellfish are filter feeders, they can contribute to cleaning the water by filtering out particulate. However, large-scale shellfish aquaculture operations can disrupt natural habitat.

An innovative new form of aquaculture, *integrated multitrophic aquaculture,* is being developed by scientists in the Bay of Fundy, New Brunswick. These scientists aim to use the relationships between complementary marine species to create synergies modelled after what happens naturally in ecosystems. That is, the byproducts of one species become fertilizers, food, and energy for another, turning natural recycling into an economic benefit. For example, an open cage filled with salmon might be placed near lines of mussels and a crop of kelp seaweed. The scientists have demonstrated that mussels and kelp then grow better, and their experiments show that organic matter residues in the mussels and kelp are always below regulatory limits. Farming these species together helps to manage the effluent from the salmon farming, and helps to save energy.

Species by Species Sustainability Guide

The sustainability of fish, shellfish, and mollusc harvests varies from year to year. The information below is based on assessments done by the David Suzuki Foundation and by SeaChoice Canada.

FISH

Freshwater fish

There are more than two hundred species of freshwater fish in Canada. The most commonly consumed include Arctic char, goldeneye, lake perch, pickerel, northern pike (also called jack-fish), trout, walleye, and whitefish. Some of these fish are subject to substantial commercial harvest. Although the commercial figures supply information about annual yields, there is no cohesive assessment available regarding the sustainability of freshwater fish. We don't know much about the ecology and habitat requirements of many freshwater species.

Scientific assessments of wild freshwater fish are being done by SeaChoice Canada, but they are not yet available for all species. We chose to include freshwater fish in this book because the issues associated with sustainability, habitat destruction, stock health, and aquaculture practices do apply to freshwater fish. Please check the SeaChoice Web site (www.seachoice.org) for future assessments of freshwater fish and updates on these species.

Arctic char

Best choice

Arctic char live in both freshwater and saltwater habitats. Most Arctic char sold in North America are farmed in land-based closed systems, with only minor risk of the cultivated fish escaping into wild waterways. There is little environmental damage associated with this method of farming.

Catfish

North American, farmed: *Best choice*

International, farmed: *Some concerns*

Most catfish available in North America are farmed. Catfish are omnivores that do not require substantial amounts of other fish in their diets, making them well suited to aquaculture. They are raised in closed-system tanks, so the chance of escape into natural waterways is low and they do not threaten wild stocks. The effluent from the farming of catfish is very carefully managed to prevent habitat damage. Catfish are often farmed in Asia using open cages, which create pollution and have a negative effect on the surrounding habitat. Catfish from Asia, which are often called basa, should be avoided.

Cod

Pacific, US, bottom.long-line, jig, trap, pot: *Best choice*

Pacific, Canada, US, trawled: *Some concerns*

Atlantic: *Avoid*

Most of the Pacific cod caught in Canada are harvested by bottom trawl, which destroys the ocean floor. If the cod are caught using other methods, such as bottom long-line, they are a great choice. Pacific cod stocks are abundant and well managed. After centuries of abundance, Atlantic cod have almost disappeared, and despite the closing of the Atlantic cod fishery, stocks have not rebounded. Scientists are working to develop cod aquaculture in the Canadian Atlantic. At this time, however, you should not eat Atlantic cod.

Dogfish

Pacific: *Some concerns*

Atlantic: *Avoid*

The dogfish population in British Columbia appears to be stable. Most dogfish are caught by long-line, which causes only minimal habitat damage and little bycatch. But dogfish mature slowly and therefore are vulnerable to overfishing. Dogfish in other regions have been severely overfished and are often harvested by bottom trawl, which can damage the ocean floor. Avoid dogfish caught outside of BC waters.

Haddock

Canada, bottom long-line: *Best choice*

US, bottom long-line: *Some concerns*; Trawled: *Avoid*

Canadian haddock caught by bottom long-line are a great choice. Trawled haddock should be avoided, as trawling destroys habitat by chewing up the ocean floor. Scientists are currently working to develop haddock aquaculture.

Hake

Pacific: *Best choice*

Pacific hake are considered to be of low conservation concern. There are two kinds of hake in British Columbia, an inshore population and a coastal population. Although the stock levels are not abundant, the fishery is given a good assessment because management controls are in place to ensure the stock is not overfished. Hake are caught by mid-water trawl, with only a low level of bycatch and has no impact on habitat.

Halibut

Atlantic, Pacific, Canada, bottom long-line: *Some concerns*

US, trawled: *Avoid*

Halibut caught by bottom long-line are generally a good choice because the stock levels are stable. There are significant concerns about the bycatch of these fisheries, and that's what knocks halibut out of the Best Choice category. Atlantic halibut caught by trawl should be avoided. Scientists are currently working to develop halibut aquaculture.

Herring

Best choice

Herring and sardine stocks are in good shape, with healthy numbers and an environmentally sustainable seine fishery. Both species are a critical part of the marine ecosystem, as they are a major source of food for other fish and marine mammals. Herring and sardines are often ground to create fish pellets, which feed carnivorous farmed fish such as salmon. A better option might be to enjoy these fish ourselves, either fresh or canned.

Lingcod

Some concerns

Most lingcod are caught by trawl, which creates some bycatch and damages habitat. A better choice is lingcod caught by hook and line, which results in little bycatch and does not damage habitat. The northern stock of lingcod is healthy at this time.

Mackerel

Best choice

Mackerel mature quickly and spawn prolifically, so they are a resilient species. In the Atlantic and the Gulf of Mexico they are caught by hook and line, which causes no habitat damage and results in little bycatch. Stock levels of mackerel are healthy.

Pollock

Best choice

Most pollock are caught by mid-water trawl, which has only a minimal habitat impact, as the nets don't touch the sea floor. Pollock stocks are currently at healthy levels; however, recent concerns about bycatch may change this assessment.

Sablefish (black cod)

Alaska, British Columbia: *Best choice*

California, Oregon, Washington: *Some concerns*

Sablefish are a good choice if they come from a Canadian fishery. Most sablefish in BC are caught by trap, a unique harvesting method that causes little habitat damage and results in little bycatch. Other acceptable methods are long-line and mid-water trawl. Bottom-trawled sablefish, however, are not a good option, as bottom-trawling damages habitat. Scientists are working to develop sablefish aquaculture.

Salmon

Pacific, wild: *Some concerns*

Farmed: *Avoid*

As wild Pacific salmon travel through almost all of British Columbia's waterways, they transport nutrients, especially when they spawn and die or are eaten by other animals. Salmon are also of enormous significance to First Nations people.

Assessing salmon stocks is complicated both because the government has reduced its assessment programs, so we're not getting as much information about the stock status, and because there are five species with different spawning times and locations. In British Columbia, we have spring (also known as chinook), sockeye, coho, pink, and chum salmon, whose populations vary considerably year to year. Some runs are much healthier than others— these days, pink and chum runs are the healthiest, and some spring runs are threatened—so it's important to know which species of salmon you're choosing and where your fish was caught. You may also want to ensure that your salmon was caught legally.

Many salmon habitats have been degraded or lost through forestry, agriculture, or development. Although salmon often travel long distances, each stock occupies only a narrow geographic area. If its habitat is disturbed, an entire stock can be lost. Climate change is also having an impact on salmon: warmer water can affect their reproduction and decrease stock levels. The good news is that Pacific salmon are fast-growing and have high reproductive potential, so the population is resilient and capable of rebounding.

All fish identified as Atlantic salmon are farmed. It is illegal to sell wild Atlantic salmon.

Farmed salmon raised in open-net cages pose a serious threat to wild salmon and the marine environment. Most farmed salmon are raised this way, and should be avoided. Even closed-tank farming is a problem: salmon are carnivorous and the production of feed for farmed salmon puts pressure on global fish stocks.

There are plans for closed-tank facilities in British Columbia that address these concerns; they will represent a fundamental and welcome change in the farmed salmon industry. These systems could be recommended on a case-by-case basis.

Sardines
See Herring.

Sturgeon Caviar
North American, farmed: *Best choice*
North American, wild: *Avoid*;
Russian, Iranian, wild: *Avoid*

Most sturgeon farmed in North America are farmed in closed-system tanks and do not endanger wild stocks or cause environmental damage. Avoid wild sturgeon from North America, which are at risk from overfishing and are caught using fishing methods that destroy habitat.

Swordfish
Atlantic, Canada, harpoon: *Best choice*
US, Atlantic, pelagic long-line: *Some concerns*
Canada, Mediterranean, Southeast Atlantic, pelagic long-line: *Avoid*

Catching swordfish by harpoon is a sustainable method; there is no bycatch and no habitat damage associated with this fishery. Stocks were depleted due to long-line fishing but are now recovering. The pelagic long-line swordfish fishery creates bycatch concerns: turtles and seabirds are attracted to the bait, get caught on the hooks, and drown.

Tilapia
North American, farmed: *Best choice*
Chinese, Taiwanese, farmed: *Avoid*

Tilapia are native to Africa and the Middle East, but they are one of the most widely distributed exotic fish in the world. Tilapia are well suited to aquaculture because they are omnivorous and don't require substantial fish protein in their feed, so they don't drag on other marine resources. Farming tilapia in open nets and cages or in raceways can endanger wild stocks, and the effluent can cause pollution. These concerns are reduced by farming in closed ponds or tanks, where the effluent can be treated or used in agriculture. Tilapia aquaculture in Asia is cause for concern in terms of environmental damage due to effluent and the possibility of farmed stock escaping into natural waters.

Trout

Rainbow, farmed: *Best choice*
Steelhead, inland farmed: *Best choice*
Wild: *See Freshwater Fish, page 167*

In Canada, rainbow trout are native only to the Pacific coast and drainages west of the Rocky Mountains. While most trout live in fresh water, steelhead trout are a saltwater variety. Beginning in the late 1880s, trout were introduced throughout the country, and lakes were stocked for sport fishing. Although trout are carnivorous, farming them does not require using substantial marine resources as feed. Trout are farmed in raceways, and the water is treated to reduce the effluent before it is returned to natural waterways. Hook-and-line fishing for trout in stocked lakes is also a good choice.

Tuna

Troll-caught: *Best choice*
US, pelagic long-line: *Some concerns*
Pacific, international, pelagic long-line: *Avoid*
Bluefin: *Avoid*

The sustainability of tuna varies depending on the kind of tuna you're choosing and how they are caught. If you're buying canned tuna, albacore and skipjack are generally good choices. Try to find the dolphin-friendly brands, which means the tuna has been caught using nets that don't trap dolphins and other bycatch. If you're buying fresh tuna, albacore, bigeye, skipjack, and yellowfin are all good choices, if they have been caught by troll or pole. Tuna caught by pelagic long-line is a fishery with serious bycatch problems. Bluefin tuna, which is critically overfished, should be avoided. If you're ordering sushi, ask the chef what kind of tuna he or she is serving and choose something else if it's bluefin. Mackerel makes a good substitute for tuna.

SHELLFISH AND MOLLUSCS

Clams

Farmed: *Best choice*

Atlantic, soft shell: *Some concerns*

Pacific, geoduck: *Some concerns*

Atlantic, dredged: *Avoid*

Most clams are farmed in clam beds on beaches and harvested by dredging small areas, which limits habitat destruction. Clams are filter feeders, so they can actually help to keep water clean. Wild clams can also be a good choice, depending on the method of harvest. Avoid clams that have been harvested using widespread hydraulic dredging, which destroys the ocean floor. Because geoduck clams are slow-growing, this species is more vulnerable to overfishing and should be consumed in moderation. Geoduck are also farmed in British Columbia, and these are a good choice.

Crab

Dungeness: *Best choice*

Alaskan king, snow: *Some concerns*

Russian king: *Avoid*

Dungeness crabs from the Pacific Northwest are a great choice; the crabs are harvested using traps, with little bycatch and no harm to the marine environment. There are concerns about stock levels of king crab in Alaska, and Russian king crabs are severely overfished and should be avoided. Snow crab stocks are vulnerable due to overfishing but the Canadian fishery is well managed, putting limits on catch totals and minimum size requirements.

Crayfish

US, farmed: *Best choice*

International, farmed: *Avoid*

Wild: *See Freshwater Fish, page 167*

Crayfish farmed in the US are considered to be a good choice. It's important that the farmed varieties don't escape into the wild; since this is a common problem with the farming techniques in countries such as China, avoid internationally farmed crayfish. There are crayfish in many lakes across Canada: some of them are native species, others are invasive species that have been introduced to natural waterways. Wild crayfish may also be available in some Canadian fish stores or farmer's markets.

Lobster

Atlantic Canada: *Best choice*

Atlantic US: *Some concerns*

Rock, spiny, US, Australia, Western Baja: *Best choice*

Spiny, international: *Avoid*

Most lobsters are caught with traps, a method of harvest that creates little habitat damage. There are only low levels of bycatch associated with the Canadian lobster fishery and stock levels are healthy.

Mussels

Farmed: *Best choice*

Wild: *Some concerns*

Mussels are a best choice as long as they're farmed. As mussels are filter feeders, they can help to keep the water clean. They can be grown on long ropes suspended in the water, causing little environmental damage, and they can also be grown on the sea floor and harvested using dredges. Even when dredged, the environmental effect is minor because the harvest is restricted to small areas. Wild-caught mussels are dredged on a larger scale, and that raises concern about habitat destruction.

Octopus

British Columbia: *Best choice*

US: *Some concerns*

Giant Pacific octopuses from British Columbia are a good choice, as the stock appears healthy and the catch rates are low. Octopuses are harvested by divers without causing harm to the marine environment. Octopus harvesters are required to collect scientific information about these creatures as a condition of their licence. The fishery is well managed, with some areas completely off-limits to fishing.

Oysters

Farmed: *Best choice*
Wild: *Some concerns*

Both American and Pacific oysters are farmed and both are a great choice: farming oysters doesn't cause environmental damage or harm wild stocks. Oysters are farmed on the beach in cultured beds where, because they are filter feeders, they can help to clean the water. Wild oysters, however, can be more of a problem, depending on how they are harvested. Dredging for oysters destroys the ocean floor; using tongs is better but still disrupts the habitat and breaks the ecosystem's food chain.

Prawns

See Shrimp.

Scallops

Farmed: *Best choice*
Wild, dive-caught: *Best choice*
Wild, dredged: *Avoid*

Scallops are farmed using trays or ropes suspended in the water, which causes little environmental damage. They can also be grown on the sea floor and harvested by dredging small areas, which limits the environmental damage to a specific location. If you're buying wild scallops, try to determine how they were harvested, and where. Most Pacific scallops are dive-caught, which makes them an excellent choice. Wild Atlantic scallops are likely to be harvested by widespread dredging, which causes significant damage to the ocean floor. These should be avoided.

Sea urchin

Best choice

The sea urchin fishery is well managed and all stocks are healthy. Divers harvest urchins by hand with no bycatch and no harm to the marine environment.

Shrimp

Trap-caught: *Best choice*

Trawled: *Some concerns*

Warm-water shrimp, Tiger prawns: *Avoid*

Pacific sidestripe shrimp and spot prawns caught by trap are both great choices; the fisheries are well managed, stocks are healthy, and the traps cause little habitat damage or bycatch. There is a growing shrimp fishery in Atlantic Canada, where the trap-caught shrimp from Canso, Nova Scotia, are also a best choice. Harvesting cold-water shrimp by trawl creates concern about habitat destruction. Warm-water shrimp and tiger prawns harvested by trawl result in critical levels of bycatch and severe habitat destruction and should be avoided.

The farming of tropical shrimp has caused extensive habitat damage in many parts of the world, including China, Thailand, and Brazil. For instance, the construction of shrimp ponds in mangrove forests has destroyed more than 37,000 hectares of coastal habitat.

Squid

Pacific: *Best choice*

Atlantic: *Some concerns*

Harvesting squid by trawl creates bycatch concerns. Much of the Atlantic squid catch is harvested using bottom-trawling methods but takes place on sandy habitats that are relatively resilient. Pacific squid are largely fished for use as bait for the sablefish, crab, and halibut fisheries. Squid are mostly caught by seine nets in British Columbia. Stocks are highly variable, as squid live only a few years, but current stock levels are generally thought to be good.

Metric Conversions

(rounded off to the nearest whole number)

WEIGHT

IMPERIAL OR U.S.	METRIC
1 oz	30 g
2 oz	60 g
3 oz	85 g
4 oz	115 g
5 oz	140 g
6 oz	170 g
7 oz	200 g
8 oz (1/2 lb)	225 g
9 oz	255 g
10 oz	285 g
11 oz	310 g
12 oz	340 g
13 oz	370 g
14 oz	400 g
15 oz	425 g
16 oz (1 lb)	455 g
2 lbs	910 g

VOLUME

IMPERIAL OR U.S.	METRIC
1/8 tsp	0.5 mL
1/4 tsp	1 mL
1/2 tsp	2.5 mL
3/4 tsp	4 mL
1 tsp	5 mL
1 Tbsp	15 mL
1/8 cup	30 mL
1/4 cup	60 mL
1/3 cup	80 mL
1/2 cup	120 mL
2/3 cup	160 mL
3/4 cup	180 mL
1 cup	240 mL
1 qt	960 mL

LIQUID MEASURES (FOR ALCOHOL)

IMPERIAL OR U.S.	METRIC
1 oz	30 mL
1 1/2 oz	45 mL

BAKING UTENSILS

IMPERIAL OR U.S.	METRIC
9-inch pie plate	23 cm pie plate

LINEAR			OVEN TEMPERATURE	
IMPERIAL OR U.S.	METRIC		IMPERIAL OR U.S.	METRIC
⅛ inch	3 mm		110°F	43°C
¼ inch	6 mm		120°F	49°C
½ inch	12 mm		125°F	52°C
¾ inch	2 cm		130°F	54°C
1 inch	2.5 cm		135°F	57°C
1¼ inches	3 cm		140°F	60°C
1½ inches	3.5 cm		145°F	63°C
1¾ inches	4.5 cm		150°F	66°C
2 inches	5 cm		155°F	68°C
3 inches	7.5 cm		160°F	71°C
4 inches	10 cm		165°F	74°C
5 inches	12.5 cm		170°F	77°C
6 inches	15 cm		175°F	79°C
7 inches	18 cm		180°F	82°C
8 inches	20 cm		200°F	93°C
9 inches	23 cm		250°F	120°C
10 inches	25 cm		300°F	150°C
11 inches	27.5 cm		325°F	160°C
12 inches	30 cm		350°F	180°C
13 inches	33 cm		360°F	182°C
14 inches	36 cm		375°F	190°C
15 inches	38 cm		400°F	200°C
16 inches	40 cm		425°F	220°C
			450°F	230°C
			475°F	245°C

Index

The David Suzuki Foundation

The David Suzuki Foundation works through science and education to protect the diversity of nature and our quality of life, now and for the future.

With a goal of achieving sustainability within a generation, the Foundation collaborates with scientists, business and industry, academia, government, and non-governmental organizations. We seek the best research to provide innovative solutions that will help build a clean, competitive economy that does not threaten the natural services that support all life.

The Foundation is a federally registered independent charity, which is supported with the help of over fifty thousand individual donors across Canada and around the world. We invite you to become a member or make a donation. For more information on how you can support our work, please contact us:

THE DAVID SUZUKI FOUNDATION
2211 West 4th Avenue, Suite 219
Vancouver, BC
Canada V6K 4S2

www.davidsuzuki.org
contact@davidsuzuki.org

Tel: 604-732-4228
Fax: 604-732-0752

Cheques can be made payable to the David Suzuki Foundation. All donations are tax-deductible.

Canadian charitable registration: (BN) 12775 6716 RR0001

U.S. charitable registration: #94-3204049